THE POCKET IDIOT'S GUIDE TO

Breaking Up

by Laurie A. Helgoe, Ph.D.

ALPHA

A member of Penguin Group (USA) Inc.

ALPHA BOOKS

Published by the Penguin Group

Penguin Group (USA) Inc., 375 Hudson Street, New York, New York 10014, U.S.A.

Penguin Group (Canada), 10 Alcorn Avenue, Toronto, Ontario, Canada M4V 3B2 (a division of Pearson Penguin Canada Inc.)

Penguin Books Ltd, 80 Strand, London WC2R 0RL, England

Penguin Ireland, 25 St Stephen's Green, Dublin 2, Ireland (a division of Penguin Books Ltd)

Penguin Group (Australia), 250 Camberwell Road, Camberwell, Victoria 3124, Australia (a division of Pearson Australia Group Pty Ltd)

Penguin Books India Pvt Ltd, 11 Community Centre, Panchsheel Park, New Delhi—110 017, India

Penguin Group (NZ), cnr Airborne and Rosedale Roads, Albany, Auckland 1310, New Zealand (a division of Pearson New Zealand Ltd)

Penguin Books (South Africa) (Pty) Ltd, 24 Sturdee Avenue, Rosebank, Johannesburg 2196, South Africa

Penguin Books Ltd, Registered Offices: 80 Strand, London WC2R 0RL, England

International Standard Book Number: 1-59257-570-6
Library of Congress Catalog Card Number: 2006929116

08 07 06   8 7 6 5 4 3 2 1

Interpretation of the printing code: The rightmost number of the first series of numbers is the year of the book's printing; the rightmost number of the second series of numbers is the number of the book's printing. For example, a printing code of 06-1 shows that the first printing occurred in 2006.

Printed in the United States of America

Note: This publication contains the opinions and ideas of its author. It is intended to provide helpful and informative material on the subject matter covered. It is sold with the understanding that the author and publisher are not engaged in rendering professional services in the book. If the reader requires personal assistance or advice, a competent professional should be consulted.

The author and publisher specifically disclaim any responsibility for any liability, loss, or risk, personal or otherwise, which is incurred as a consequence, directly or indirectly, of the use and application of any of the contents of this book.

Most Alpha books are available at special quantity discounts for bulk purchases for sales promotions, premiums, fund-raising, or educational use. Special books, or book excerpts, can also be created to fit specific needs.

For details, write: Special Markets, Alpha Books, 375 Hudson Street, New York, NY 10014.

To Barron, who has made me grateful for every breakup before him.

Contents

Appendixes

Introduction

Breaking up is something we spend a lot of energy avoiding. We stay in bad relationships, we cling to someone who's distant, or we just try, try, try. Even when the writing is on the wall (and the e-mail and the voicemail), we delude ourselves into thinking there's more we can do. Then, when reality hits and the door closes, it's no wonder we feel broken and ready to fall apart!

Hold the phone! Don't call and jump back into avoidance. This book takes the isolation and mystery out of breaking up—whether you're the one dumping or the one being dumped. There are predictable feelings everyone goes through, responses that help and responses that hurt—and there are ways to make life better again.

Beyond getting through, this book helps you overcome the avoidance that leaves you feeling helpless. As weird as this sounds right now, getting a handle on breaking up will help you approach new relationships and become more powerful than ever! So turn off that phone, sit down with this book, and let's break down breaking up. Meanwhile, you get to stay in one piece.

Extras

Sidebars are included throughout this book to give you a bit more to work with. These little extras will give you food for thought, tidbits to lighten your load, and some solid advice to keep you strong.

Breakup Repair

These boxes are filled with ideas and exercises to help you get through, rise above, and move beyond the breakup blues.

Lonely Street

The warnings in these boxes will keep you from adding more pain to the breakup game.

Breakup Bytes

These boxes provide interesting and entertaining trivia about breaking up, help you feel less alone, and might even make you laugh.

Acknowledgments

Thanks to Lori Gibson, whose insight and literary voice has frequently inspired me.

To Becca, my muse: Thanks for walking the walk and asking for more.

To Cindy Boggs: Thanks for your suggestions, help, and ongoing support, and for letting me hide out at your place so I could get this done!

To Tracy Williams: Thanks for your ideas and your talent at expressing them. Thanks also to Krista Holcomb for your creative suggestions.

To Joshua: Thanks for coming up with a great way for us to spend my advance. The rain forest awaits!

To Jacky Sach, my agent, and Randy Ladenheim-Gil, my editor: Thank you for your help, knowledge, and professionalism. I appreciate the way things flow when I'm working with the two of you!

The Breakup Blues: It's Over!

In This Chapter

- Understanding why it hurts
- No more "should"-ing on yourself
- Identifying sources of sadness
- Diagnosing your breakup and your blues
- Getting motivated to get through

Ouch! There's no doubt about it: breaking up hurts. Whether you're doing the breaking up or getting it done to you, it stinks. You can tell yourself, "It's for the best" all you want to, but when it feels like the world as you knew it just exploded, you'd just as soon put "for the best" right down the garbage disposal.

It doesn't matter if you like the guy or not, breaking up is everything you despise in life: rejection, loneliness, insecurity, fear, worry—just generally feeling like crap about yourself. And the bad feelings don't stop there: you've got the longings for the ex, hatred of the ex, anger (okay, rage), jealousy …. You get the point. Breaking up stirs us up like nothing else, inspiring hit songs and 10-tissue chick flicks. It's a big deal, whether we want it to be or not.

Not only are post-breakup feelings messy, but they also can really mess you up. Do you find yourself asking, "Why didn't I see this coming? What's wrong with me? Why am I so depressed all the time?" So not only are you feeling bad, but you're feeling bad about feeling bad!

So what's best? Indulge in misery and Haagen Dazs, or buck up and force ourselves to move on? Let's deal with moving on later. In this chapter, we're going to take a look at the mess of emotions that come with a breakup, not so we can judge them, but so that we can understand and accept them. We'll also do some sorting to reduce the mess. This chapter is about being right where we are—allowing the feelings, hugging them, giving them a playroom. This is the heart of the drama. Relish the aliveness of feeling deeply.

Where's the Course on THIS?

So if breaking up is such a big deal, why don't we get some training in it? Like many matters of the heart, we all assume we should just *know*. Or that learning about love and loss would take the mystery away and pop the bubble of romance. For whatever reason, smart and cool grownups though we may be, we find ourselves clueless, relentlessly asking why and then beating ourselves up for being so obsessed.

A course might help us deconstruct these thoughts. Do the following statements sound familiar?

- "I was a wreck when we were together. I should be happy we broke up!"
- "He was a jerk." (Repeat "*should*" statement)
- "If he doesn't want me, I *should*n't want him."
- "I *should* have seen this coming! What's wrong with me?"

See how we *should* all over ourselves? The "s" word is a great clue that we're being mean to ourselves, acting like we're really stupid for being the way we are. But we don't stop there: we even call ourselves choice names like "pathetic" and "loser." It is amazing how, at the times we are hurting most, we are capable of turning against ourselves. Rather than soothing the wound of the breakup, we rub salt right in and continue to pound on ourselves. Let's stop the beatings right now! It's time to get some understanding.

A course would show us that breakup feelings are rarely just about the breakup. Separation can trigger old feelings of loss or abandonment. This is why we can feel devastated after breaking up with someone we aren't even that wild about (sound familiar?). When I feel rejected, my brain thinks I'm back in grade school, being told I'm not wanted on the softball team. We all have sad stories about being ignored, left out or just plain left, facing scary changes and losing something important, from our favorite Barbie to our first boyfriend.

If you watch the video of Kelly Clarkson's hit song, "Because of You," you can see this blend of old and new feelings. The images move between current scenes of a fight with her man and past scenes of the father who ignored and then left her. At first, her feelings seem to be about the fight, then about her father, but ultimately focus on her mother who taught her to "play it safe."

So what would your video look like? Are your feelings really about the present breakup, or does it trigger some old hurt you never really dealt with?

 Breakup Repair

> Every time you slip into being mean to yourself, say you're sorry and turn the tables. For example, "I'm such a loser" needs a grand gesture. Nominate yourself for an Oscar or Nobel Prize and list the unique qualities that make *you* the winner. Don't forget your acceptance speech! Other ideas might include a love letter to you, hugging yourself or a favorite stuffed animal, giving yourself a warm bath…or maybe an even warmer burst of erotic pleasure.

When you're the one dumped, feelings can go way beyond missing the relationship. One of the hardest things is that you don't have control over the decision. It seems every sitcom runs an episode about being in this position (as if it's funny!). Usually the main character, let's call her Jane, wants to break up with her boyfriend (Dick, naturally). She gets up her nerve and tells Dick, "We need to talk." Dick then says, "Yes, I have something I need to talk to you about, too," and then says he wants to break up. Rather than feeling relieved, Jane is devastated. What happened? Jane lost her position of control. The loss of control is what she's upset about—it has nothing to do with losing the relationship!

Clearing Emotional Clutter

When feelings get too messy, we get anxious. And when we get anxious, we feel pressured and frantic. We can start to scare ourselves into thinking that we're not okay. So a first step in embracing our feelings is to de-clutter. Think of how good you feel after sorting your closet and getting rid of all the stuff you don't use. Sorting old feelings from new and putting feelings where they belong can also leave us feeling lighter and more in control.

Writing your feelings is a great way to clear emotional space and sort feelings. Here's a simple strategy:

Take a piece of paper and write down everything you're feeling and thinking. Don't worry about punctuation or writing complete sentences; just get it out. If swear words best capture the intensity of your feelings, use them. If the feeling reminds you of old stuff, write that, too. Don't worry whether it makes sense. Write at least a page and keep going until it's all out.

Now, go back through and circle anything that is mean. Cover this writing up with a sad face and say you're sorry. These are lies and you don't want them in your closet.

Next, circle anything that is old and done with, overused or boring, and write "EXPIRED" over it.

Look at what's left and ask if it's true. Watch for paranoid conclusions ("Everybody hates me," which is also mean), overstatements ("I'm going crazy!" which is also mean) and unfounded predictions ("I'll never find anyone," which is also mean). Find these lies and put a slash through them.

You've just cleared your closet! As we move through this chapter, we'll continue to sort and break down the rubble of breaking up.

Varieties of Breakups

If I tell you, "I just went through a breakup," you're going to want to know more. That's because *how* a breakup happens makes a big difference in what we're feeling. And, let's face it, we all like a good story.

Every breakup has two stories, one for each participant. Although we would probably agree that it's better to dump than to be dumped, it's a myth that being the initiator comes without hurt. Often, we break up with someone *because* we've been hurt or disappointed by the other. The difference—and it's an important one—is that the initiator has control over the timing. The one hanging in there may have come to the same conclusion given more time.

We'll talk about the down-side of having the control in Chapter 2.

Let's look at some common breakup plots:

Life

Sometimes a relationship is good, but life happens. These breakups are the result of divergent life choices. Examples include, *I'm going away to college—you want to stay near family. You want to work on your career—I want to hitchhike cross-country.*

Feelings can range from bittersweet to tragic, depending on how close the relationship was. The dramatic theme is, *Impossible choice.*

Timing

These breakups happen when the two of you are in different places in your life journey and can't find a way to meet. This can be due to age or maturity differences (*not* the same thing!) or differences in relationship history. Examples include, *You're ready to get serious—I'm not. I'm ready to move out of my parents' basement and have a social life—you're not.*

Feelings range from disappointment to exasperation, depending on how accepting you both are of the differences. The dramatic theme is, *Right place, wrong time.*

Values

A clash of values can be another reason for breaking up, especially when the value is central to your identity. Examples include, *We worship differently. I like to drink—you won't. I date one person at a time—you don't.*

Feelings can be bittersweet and tragic or angry and indignant, depending on how offensive you find the conflicting values. The dramatic theme is, *We can't see eye to eye.*

Another Love

This is a particularly painful type of breakup that happens when one of you finds (or longs for) another. Examples include, *You love that airheaded, silicone-enhanced bimbo. My heart still belongs to my high-school sweetheart.*

Feelings explode with this type of breakup and may include anything from anger to murderous rage; guilt and self-loathing when you're the cheater; envy, competitiveness, and inferiority toward the other; and feeling hurt, betrayed, or abandoned. The intensity of feelings and theme of sadness vs. anger will vary depending on whether the dumper was upfront or deceptive and dishonest about the feelings, and whether he or you actually cheated. One of the nastiest things about betrayal is that it stomps on your sense of trust, which can be challenging to get back. Dramatic theme is, *Jilted.*

Conflict

These breakups happen when conflict begins to dominate the relationship. Your personalities grate, you fight a lot, and despite your efforts, you can't seem to meet each other's needs. You may find yourself saying, "Does a relationship need to be this much work?!" A cost-benefit analysis reveals that the two of you are in the red. Yet, conflict can be a weird sort of glue. In high-conflict relationships, the biggest challenge can be giving up the fight—especially if you have great make-up sex!

Feelings of anger, hurt from fights, and frustration dominate such breakups. You can also feel a sense of failure once you admit that you can't (or don't want to) work out the conflict. Dramatic theme is, *Losing battle, cutting your losses.*

Chemical Imbalance

These are the breakups that are hard to explain: the garden-variety, "It's not you—it's me" breakups. As much as you like each other, one or both of you feels something is missing. Whether you call it chemistry, soul connection, or that "in love" feeling, the relationship is missing a special something that you need.

These breakups can be hard to initiate because there aren't any tangible reasons to give, and they're hard to receive for the same reason. You may be tempted to believe that there's more to it. When one of you feels it and the other doesn't, the outcome can be very painful for the one who thought it was The One. Dramatic theme is, *Unrequited love.*

Unsolved Mystery

The toughest breakups are often the ones that aren't acknowledged—he just stops calling or answering calls or keeps you hanging with sweet nothings as he boards a plane to Siberia. As a friend of mine put it, "He wasn't there to even see what he'd done to me!"

These breakups are hard to resolve because you have so little information, or what he's saying to you doesn't fit what he's doing. (He's saying he still loves you, but calling from another woman's apartment.) So it's easy to talk yourself into any explanation, depending on how up you are for self-deception. You're probably feeling confused, preoccupied, and abandoned, while also holding a well of hurt and anger that has nowhere to go. Dramatic theme is, *Dazed and confused.*

 Lonely Street

> We know that calling the ex is a really bad idea. If he's sweet, we feel worse. If he's mean, we feel worse. If we go off on him, we feel worse. And every time we call, we give away more of that remaining thread of self-esteem. And yet it's *sooooo* tempting! So get your friends ready to remind you of the 5,000 reasons it's a bad idea to call. When you feel the temptation, call them instead.

Try writing out your breakup story as if it's a movie. Step back and appreciate its dramatic value. What do you want for your character? What has she learned? What would make the best ending?

Beyond Blue: The Feeling Spectrum

Though we usually associate breaking up with the blues, a breakup can trigger a whole kaleidoscope of feelings on the color spectrum. Now you can add color-coding as you sort your feeling closet. Get one of those huge boxes of Crayolas and color over expressions of feeling with the matching shade. Watch your emotional world come to life. What are your breakup colors? Here are some of the common ones:

Red

Getting mad is a common response to a breakup, especially when there's betrayal or abuse involved. Anger can be tough because your ex isn't around to lash out at, and you're really not interested in becoming a stalker. (No, you're not.) It doesn't work to keep it in either. When anger gets turned on yourself, the red can turn blue.

Gray

We might have the "blahs" after a breakup, not really feeling much of anything. Why feel? It hurts too much. If the blahs evolve into day after day in bed, loss of interest in everything (including shopping), then we've moved beyond gray to a colorless depression. Here's when feeling blue is progress. Get a therapist, Prozac prescription, or both, and let the tears flow!

Green

As we discussed, envy is natural when another person becomes the focus of the ex's attention. It is also common to feel jealous of couples who are happy, and we may find ourselves temporarily distancing ourselves from them. We are often uncomfortable admitting envy, yet this emotion can give us clues to what we want for ourselves.

Yellow

Fear can also be in the picture after a breakup. We may feel afraid of venturing out and risking a new relationship. If you felt really passionate about your ex, you might "play it safe" and date someone who is safer but less exciting. Problem is, you then replace the risk of loss with the *guarantee* of boredom.

Black and White

We can become negative and cynical, or indulge in behaviors we didn't formerly approve of. It's our way of trying to show the world (and ourselves) that we don't care. Scratch the black and we'll probably find blue. We can go in the white direction as well, convincing ourselves that we're pure and faultless victims, and the ex is pure evil. (Well, that *could* be true ….)

Peachy

Wedged in between all those crummy feelings, you might find a part of yourself that feels just fine—maybe even better than fine. Feelings of relief, strength, and peace can surprise you in the middle of the worst situations.

It Seemed So Right

Even when things get really bad in a relationship, even when the couple agrees that it's best to part, it's tough to say goodbye. We don't stay in bad relationships because we enjoy punishment. It's the good stuff—or memories of good stuff—that we hate to let go. We may even catch ourselves repeating that overused phrase, "It seemed so right!"

Remember when it seemed right? This is when we tend to suffer a little brain damage. That "right" feeling is incredibly powerful. We don't want it to end. So our minds build stories. We see ourselves continuing in this bliss, and we can't imagine things going wrong. When things do go wrong—even *very* wrong, we refuse to see it.

Sometimes, the relationship we're mourning was over long before the breakup. Some people hold on to a bad relationship because of the blissful beginning. Others jump from beginning to beginning, never staying in one relationship long enough to find out what's really there. But whether we're jumping or holding, we are glued to an illusion.

Meanwhile, we miss out on opportunities for satisfaction and contentment that *doesn't* fizzle out after the first few dates.

Discovering Breakup Blessings

Because of the tendency to hang on to things that were once good, breaking up (even being dumped!) can ultimately be a blessing. A breakup ends the wishing for something where there is nothing (or at least not enough). As long as we're caught up in the illusion, we cannot begin to replace it with something real.

This book is here to help you face and conquer the challenges of breaking up. We put a lot of energy into developing relationship skills, but we can also develop breaking-up skills. Having these skills—not just at initiating a breakup, but also at accepting the ones we don't initiate—can help us have more courage to sample relationships, discover what we like and don't like, and ultimately find what we're really looking for.

The Least You Need to Know

- Accept your feelings even if they don't make sense.
- Avoid using *should statements* on yourself.
- Separate old baggage from new feelings.
- Get specific about what you're feeling.
- Consider that your distress may *not* be about losing this relationship.

Chapter 2

Calling It Quits

In This Chapter

- Addressing obstacles to breaking it off
- Why "decision" is better than "answer"
- Accepting responsibility
- The downside of "nice"
- Following through

You know the relationship isn't any fun anymore. In fact, it's really bringing you down. Then why is it so hard to call it quits? The same skills that make you good at relationships can make it hard to end them. And just when you think you're ready, a little voice of self-doubt chimes in with a quivering, "What if you can't find anyone else?" Then comes the guilty backup, "How can you *do* this?" Before long, a rap war of inner voices is mucking up your thinking.

If we don't like making decisions or using the "no" word—or are just too nice—breaking up can feel like a ridiculous yoga pose. At the same time, the stretch might be just what we need to build some muscle. Remember, if you can't say, "No," then you can't really say, "Yes," either. So let's work on that "no."

This chapter will help you get clear and stay clear in the face of inner and outer static, so you can do what needs to be done. We'll talk about the temptation to keep trying, fears about making a mistake, discomfort with being the "bad guy," concerns about your ex, and that way-overused feeling of guilt. Once you work all that through, you may not only feel stronger, but pounds lighter!

From "Try" to Goodbye

You're waiting in an endless line for concert tickets. To pass the time, you chat with the guy next to you. Just before you reach the booth, he asks you to lunch. You have a slow week, so you say, "Why not?" He treats you to a nice lunch; you have an okay time. You discuss a new movie you both want to see. He suggests you go together. Hmm, a real date. Again: "Why not?"

One date leads to another and, before long, you're dating. You wake up one morning and it hits you: "What happened?" You don't want to be in this relationship! Then the chorus begins: "But he's such a nice guy, maybe I should try harder, why am I so picky?" Now fully brainwashed, you decide that you'll try harder on your next date. You get a new shirt, wear your sexy perfume, and ask him more about his work.

Things do go a little better. The voice inside your head says, "See?" and you reluctantly schedule another date.

Sound familiar? The challenge of breaking up is that *there is always more that you can do.* Whether your relationship is ho-hum like the one above, or whether you've run into conflict that is making you miserable, it's easy to stay in perpetual "try harder" mode.

A similar trap is to keep looking for the right "answer," as if some logic-based formula will reveal the ultimate truth. Truth is, every decision comes with loss and gain. There is no way to do a breakup without getting your hands a little dirty. And as clear as you are, there will be good arguments for the other choice. Making the call is hard. So, you stew and wring your hands, waiting for the sky to open up with that answer.

An alternative is to say to yourself: "Yes, there is more I can do, but I'm choosing not to do more. There are arguments for staying, but I'm choosing to go. I've decided to end the relationship."

The Courage to Give Up

The "more I can do" mentality works like gambling: You've already pumped the machine with lots of quarters, and you think, "Maybe if I just keep at it a little longer, I'll hit the jackpot." So, after another run to the cash machine, you start dropping more money in. Now it's harder to quit, because you've put more on the line and you don't want to acknowledge losing.

Similarly, the investment of time and emotion in a relationship make it hard to pull out.

Just as it takes guts to stop gambling when you've lost money, it takes courage to give up on a losing relationship. Giving up means facing that it didn't work, that the investment didn't pay off.

Let's take the gambling idea a step further. If you're incredibly wealthy, you may not worry that much about throwing money on the table then walking away. The gambling is entertainment, not a way of making money. But if you're broke, it hurts to lose that money.

Likewise, if you're feeling hard up for a relationship, you'll be more tempted to hang on. The thinking is, *"What if there's no one else out there?"* What we forget is, we've already lost. Here are some exercises to help you walk away:

- **Keep a record of your losses.** Jot down every loss you experience by being in the relationship. Maybe it's an evening lost to a bad date, it might be self-esteem or confidence lost because you just got yelled at or put down; maybe you lose yourself a little each time your date controls what you do.

- **Entertain other options.** As you note the losses, write what you would prefer to be doing and who you'd prefer to be with, even if the answer is "by myself" or a description of someone you haven't met yet.

- **Start earning more "*date value*."** Do what you need to do to feel like you've got options. Get a makeover, start working out, take a class to make yourself more interesting. (Knowing massage can be a great asset!) If you feel broke emotionally, see a therapist.

- **Take pride in giving up.** Do what comedians do: boldly overstate the bad news. You don't need to stand up in a bar, but you can look in the mirror and say, "Yup, I give up. I'm clueless about how to make this work. I declare this relationship an utter and total failure."

 Breakup Repair

To build up your breakup muscles, identify other bad investments and give them up. If you are losing sleep over a project that someone else could complete more easily, hand it off. If you have a shirt you spent a lot of money on but never wear, give it away. As you give up on what's not working, you free up energy to go after what you want.

Once you step out of the relationship, it usually gets easier. You may even find yourself saying, "Wow. I should have done this months ago!" But please don't beat yourself up about that. You have done it and you're free!

Being the Bad Guy

Few of us like to be the bad guy, especially those of us who aren't guys. Girls are experts in making things right in relationships, not breaking them up. How many times have you found yourself trying to please a person you don't even *like*? Breaking up goes against our nature.

Well, it just may be time to improve on nature. Let's look at the problems with being "nice," and how being the bad guy may sometimes be the kindest way.

Sometimes Nice Is Insulting

Take it from me, being a caretaker has a dark side. Have you ever found yourself protecting someone else's feelings because you secretly see that person as weak? Would you like to be seen that way?

A clue to problem caretaking is when we aren't being nice out of genuine desire, but because we feel sorry for the person. Feeling sorry puts us in a one-up position, and is ultimately insulting.

Sometimes Nice Is Dishonest

If we want to break up, nice behavior can be a lie. We may think we're sparing the other person pain, but maybe it's our own discomfort we are sparing. We want to be seen a certain way (good, kind) and, of course, we *have* to be liked! The focus on how we are seen pulls us further and further away from the truth and adds more to undo in the end. (Think about a maddening scene in a sitcom where the dumper wimps out and proposes instead!)

Sometimes Nice Is Controlling

How many of you operate on this rule: "If I'm nice, then he's supposed to be nice"? (My hand is raised.) Sometimes we're nice because we don't want to face the ex's feelings. We want it smooth and easy. What fairyland are we living in?! Notice the "breaking" in breaking up? By definition, he's going to feel differently than you. And if your ex gets mad or hurt, that's his right. As long as he isn't abusive (self-protection always comes first), he has a right to feel whatever he feels.

That doesn't mean you need to take care of his feelings, which may just be another way of trying to control them, but you can acknowledge them, say you're sorry he has to go through this, and say goodbye. Of course, there's another possibility here: Maybe, just maybe, he'll be fine! (Pause for the ego deflation.)

Sometimes Nice Is Bad for You

The biggest rip-off about playing nice is that it deprives you of your power. You know how you get that edge when you're PMS-ing and suddenly people are scared of you? That's power!

When we get caught up in taking care of everyone else, we miss out on the good feelings that come with taking charge, expressing our truth, and getting what we want. Instead, we act all tortured and helpless while building up the ego of the guy we want out of our lives! When we're premenstrual, we just don't have the energy for the cover-up. Here's an idea: time the breakup with your cycle!

Sometimes Nice Is Nice

As long as nice isn't getting in your way, a little dose of it is a good thing. In fact, your ability to be clear and kind shows that you are letting go. For example, you may want to thank your soon-to-be-ex for the fun you had together or for helping you learn some new things about yourself.

 Lonely Street

> Watch the temptation to say too much as you're ending it. Showing him your wounds says you want something from him. Bringing up your arguments says you're hoping to resolve them. If you have truly decided to leave, there is really very little to say.

True kindness respects a person's right to know the truth, to be treated with dignity, and to feel what he feels.

That Thing Called Guilt

Before, during, and after you break up, you'll probably get flack from inside yourself. Enter the familiar voice of guilt:

"How could you do that to him?

"Look at all he did for you!"

"Why are you so selfish?"

"Didn't you learn anything from your mother/church/ Girl Scout leader?"

The knee-jerk reaction to this inner voice is to either get defensive or give in. When we get defensive, we engage in lively internal conversations that ultimately get us nowhere (meanwhile concerning co-workers who try to get our attention). When we give in to guilt, we drag out breakups until we're walking down the aisle in a white dress.

The secret to out-foxing guilt is to agree with the inner voice: "Yes, I'm hurting a very nice guy who has been really good to me," "Yes, I'm selfish," or "You're right, my mom would probably have been much nicer." The guilt voice is telling part of the truth—the hardest part. If we don't accept that part, guilt will hook us. If we do accept the hardest part, guilt loses its power.

Setting the Stage

Here it is. Time to end it, the finale, the closing of the curtain. First, you need to set the stage:

1. If you are sharing a place—or a bed—get your things together before you talk. Save yourself the awkward post-breakup search for your panties.

2. Pick a neutral spot for "the talk." Meet somewhere that allows you a quick exit if needed. Don't depend on him for a ride, and avoid your place or his place.

   You might meet up at a park or a café during off hours. Meeting face to face is respectful, helps you both get closure, and also makes it less awkward if you run into him later. The big exception is, if his M.O. is to make a scene or become abusive, then a phone call is a reasonable alternative—you can tell him why you did it this way, and you can always hang up. Respect goes both ways. Avoid a letter or e-mail, because written words can be misconstrued and used against you.

3. Plan an exit strategy. Have something scheduled that will help you break away. It's probably too soon (and tacky) to arrange a date, but a movie with a supportive girlfriend might be just what you need.

Putting thought into the final scene will save you a lot of grief in the end. On to rehearsal.

Practice, Practice, Practice!

Use the following guidelines to make this as painless as possible. If you're nervous, run through some rehearsals with a friend:

- **Use "I" statements.** Keep the focus on yourself. "I am not happy" goes over much better than "You are a loser."

- **Be clear.** State it simply, as in, "This relationship is not working for me. I want to stop seeing each other." Don't leave him wondering with statements like, "Maybe we should back off a little."

- **Be kind ...** You can acknowledge the good qualities of the person you are breaking up with, while indicating that it just isn't the right fit for you. Though it seems cliché, the reminder that he deserves someone who is crazy about him can help. (If you think he deserves pond scum, just stay silent on the point.)

- **... but not too kind.** This *is* a breakup after all. You can acknowledge the ex's feelings, but it's not your job to put him back together. That's what moms and shrinks are for.

- **Be truthful.** Although you don't want to get hooked into explaining every problem with the relationship, you can provide some honest feedback. For example: "I want someone with more of an interest in what's going on in my world."

Okay, time to apply what we've discussed. Here's some sample dialogue to get you warmed up:

Jane: Dick, I've thought this through, and I want to end our relationship.

Dick: Whoa. Ouch. Why the hell didn't you say something before?

Jane: (Silence, looks at him with empathy.)

Dick: I thought things were going great. What happened?

Jane: You're right. A lot about our relationship was great. But I'm not happy.

Dick: How can you not be happy?! I take you out to nice restaurants, the sex is great—we have fun, don't we? What did I do wrong?

Jane: Yes, you did all that, and I have had fun with you. But I'm looking for something more. I think you know what I'm talking about.

Dick: What, more "talk"? Why is it always about talking?!

Jane: It's just what I need. But I am glad I had the chance to be with you.

Dick: Yeah, yeah. Well I'm not so "glad."

Jane: Yeah.

Dick: Listen, maybe I can change. We're talking right now, aren't we?

Jane: No. I'm saying goodbye. Dick, this is what I need.

Dick: But I don't need it. I love you!

Jane: I know, and I'm sorry, but this is what it is. I packed up the stuff I had at your place and it's in my car. I left you the photos. You may find this hard to believe, but I really do wish you the best.

Dick: You staying would be the best.

Jane: (Leaving) No, it wouldn't. You deserve someone who is crazy about you. Goodbye.

Dick: Thanks for nothing.

Jane: (No response; exits)

Note that Jane does not bite on Dick's attempts to get her to explain or feel guilty. Her silence keeps her out of the struggle while enabling him to feel what he feels. Note also that she had attended to practical matters so that she could leave free and clear. At the end, he slimes her with a parting dig: his last-ditch effort to engage her. She walks away.

While this may look simple on paper, we know that breaking up is not. There will be a tug of war between providing feedback and just saying goodbye, between being kind and being clear. Don't expect it to be clean. Just do it.

Showtime

By now, you're hopefully tired of rehearsing and just want to get it done. Don't spoil your efforts by getting drunk or high. You can do this! As you go through the breakup, allow a part of yourself to observe what happens. This is high drama and it doesn't (thankfully!) happen very often. He may throw you a few curve balls—see this as plot thickener. When in doubt, say nothing. Keep it short. Do it, and then thank yourself.

The Least You Need to Know

- Don't ask yourself if there's more you can do; ask yourself if you want to do more.
- Accept your losses.
- Trade in "nice" for honest.
- Keep the ending short.

Chapter **3**

No Means ... No?

In This Chapter

- Avoiding traps to get you back
- Can you really "be friends"?
- What to do with the stuff
- How to protect yourself

You did it! It's officially over.

Well, kind of. Except your stuff is at his place and, okay, he calls a lot. And you were lonely the other night and gave into some friendly sex. But that's it!

Why is it so hard to stick with "No"? We talked about guilt and bad-guy feelings in the last chapter. In this chapter we'll look at hooks that come from outside ourselves.

After the "talk," we can get hit by all kinds of challenges, from what to do with his toothbrush (toss it if it's not electric) to what the "ex-relationship" will be like. (Is there such a thing?) We'll talk about these practical questions, as well as how to deal with your ex's demand for detailed reasons. (Tell him you aren't licensed to do personality assessments!) As clear as your "No" may be, breaking up can be just the beginning of disentangling your life from your ex.

Parting Interrogations

"Why" questions are one of the toughest obstacles to breaking up. You've already wrestled with your "whys"; now you're getting a barrage of questions from the ex: "What went wrong? What did I do? Why can't we make it work?" And it doesn't matter if you've answered the questions or not, he doesn't get it and he wants you to tell him again.

This is where the edge we discussed in Chapter 2 will help. Think PMS! Use these reminders to keep your head straight while you decline the interrogation:

- Deep down, most people know why. If you think back, you've probably already told him everything he needs to know. Tell him you don't have anything more to add to what you've already said. Say goodbye.

- No matter how pitiful he sounds, it's not your job to put him back together. Encourage him to talk to someone, but make it clear: that person cannot be you. Say goodbye.

- Once you've laid out the boundaries, enforce them. Don't answer the phone; change your number; block his number. Remember, his need to call you reflects his desire to pull you back in. The logic is, even if you are telling him to go away, you are talking and there is still hope.

● Moving on yourself is the best way you can help him move on. He may be testing you to see if you really meant what you said. If you repeatedly stand the test, he'll get the message. (If not, proceed to "stopping stalkers" later in this chapter!)

Parting Intentions

Another tricky area is the question of how—or *if*—you will relate post-breakup. This is especially dicey when you work together or live in a small town. You can save yourself a lot of hassle if you make your intentions clear.

Line in the Sand

When a relationship has been particularly intense or conflict-ridden, the idea of staying in touch feels about as likely as Saddam and Bush cozying up. (Ooh—sorry about that image!) And we all know how insulting it feels to have the "Just Friends" sign held up by someone who sends your hormones into high gear.

When friendly contact is not an option, don't set yourself up by suggesting it. Here's where cold turkey is the most effective approach: no e-mails, no IM-ing, no phone calls, and certainly *no sleepovers!*

Similarly, a relationship that has been destructive requires clear boundaries. And when you make boundaries explicit—"I'll say 'Hi' if I see you, but will not engage in a conversation"—it is so much easier to refer back to them if he pushes them.

So what about the co-worker or small-town problem? You can go over scenarios with him and discuss how to handle them. What routines did you have together that will need to change? As nit-picky as this may seem, the more specific you can get, the more smoothly this will go. Even if you don't communicate every detail, having it clear in your own head will help you avoid mixed messages. In particularly intense relationships, a short leave of absence from work, if you can manage it, can provide a helpful cooling-off period.

Friendship

"Can we be friends?"

STOP! Before the words roll off your tongue, think about what you're asking. First of all, is this what you really want, or are you just saying it to soften the blow? If you're trying to soften the blow, you're using a sledgehammer!

The concept, while common, is not nice *or* soft. Unless the relationship started as a friendship and slipped temporary (and mistakenly) into romance, you are proposing a very lame compromise. You are basically asking, "Can we trade the excitement (and perhaps rabid lovemaking) we've had for meetings at Starbucks where I talk about men who are more attractive than you?" Face it: asking for a friendship is insulting! Although more difficult, it's much kinder to acknowledge the truth: you want this relationship to end. Period.

But maybe you really do want him as a friend. It's perfectly understandable to still want some of the positive benefits of the relationship, especially if he's a good listener or, better yet, a handyman! But here's the rub: how will it feel to have him talking about women he finds more attractive than *you*?

Face it! At least in the near-term, the two of you aren't going to call, have dinner, go shopping, and send birthday cards like you do with real friends. Though dating provides added perks, it pretty much covers the same ground as a good friendship. Unless you both simultaneously decide you prefer the other gender, the prospect of friendship muddies the waters big time. You can be "friendly," but find your friends elsewhere.

Maybe he is the one suggesting friendship. Here are some signs of a guy in friendship clothing who really still longs for you:

- He wants to discuss why the relationship didn't work.
- He wants to take you out for dinner.
- He continues to call and inquire about your life.
- He stares at you with lustful eyes.
- He lingers.
- He moves in for a kiss at the end of a "friendly" outing.

Second Chances

What if you love your ex, but broke up because of a deal-breaker (e.g., he's an alcoholic, a sex addict, a priest)? Maybe you're hoping the breakup will push him to get his act together and come back to you reformed and ready. In this case, you are establishing a boundary, but one that he *could* qualify to cross.

 Breakup Repair

> You can't count on it, but reform does happen. Many exes have later admitted (often *much* later) that being dumped was the best thing that happened to them; that others had skirted around the problem, but your breakup was the first thing that woke him up. When you refuse to participate in a partner's self-destructive behavior, you are not only taking a stand on your own behalf, but you are also performing an act of love.

Careful, girl! You treated yourself with respect by breaking the deal, but your love makes you vulnerable. The risk is that the first time your ex says, "I've really decided to change!" you run over with the keys to your apartment. People decide to change every day! (Probably as often as married guys decide to leave their wives.)

Reform does happen—otherwise I wouldn't have gone into the therapy business—but it usually takes a *lot* of breakups (and job losses, and emotional breakdowns) before they hit bottom. The big question is, do you want to wait that long?

No. That's why you broke up. So leave the second-chance idea in the category of miracles and surprises, and leave. As trite as the old butterfly saying is, this is the time to let go and trust the outcome. If he comes back in a couple years as a licensed counselor and you happen to be single, maybe the breakup did its magic. But to protect yourself, get very, very clear about what reform looks like to you, and know that it won't happen next week. (If the sky opens up to him, he'll still have work to do!)

From Our Space to My Space

When you and your ex have lived together, the breakup plot thickens. Not only do you have the challenge of separating, but you've also got to separate your stuff—and maybe even need to find a place to live! And when one of you is moving out, feelings of emptiness can be heightened. Either you are leaving a space that had become home, or his familiar presence vacates your space.

Moving Out

Get your game face on. If you've planned the breakup, you can plan the move. You can decide in advance where to go, whether it's home to Mom's or onward to a new apartment. Of course, when *you* get dumped, you are suddenly single *and* homeless. As bad as this sounds, you gain major sympathy points with friends and family, and it can be an advantage to stay with a close friend or family member while getting yourself together. Just sharing a meal with someone who cares can be wonderfully nurturing and grounding. On the other hand, it can be tough to share space, especially if you process things more internally. Here are some questions to consider as you vacate your ex's place:

- What are my options? List every possibility you can think of: people you can stay with, places you can rent, and roommate options. Be creative: maybe you want to spend one night in a luxury hotel and spa, and get personal space and pampering in one package.

- Do I need people now, or space—or a little of both?

- What kinds of support do I need close at hand? Convenience to work? Friends? Family? Church? Health club?

- Where have I always wanted to live? Consider that this may be your opportunity to have a place that really suits you.

- What can I afford?

- What do I need to do now, what can wait until tomorrow, and what requires a longer-term plan? Moving can be overwhelming, so break it down in to manageable bits.

- If I stay with someone, is it someone who "gets" me and knows what I need—and what I *don't*? Someone who would annoy me with unwelcome advice or wild kids? Or someone who'll help me move on with my life?

Once you decide where to go, take the time and pack *all* your stuff. Yes, it's hard, but having to come back or, worse, having him handle your stuff, will be harder. (A friend of mine received a box from her ex which included her clothes *as well as* his previous girlfriends' clothes!) You can ask him to leave while you pack, or you can go stay with a friend and come back when he's gone. Avoid situations where he's looking over your shoulder—or, worse, trying to *help*—as you gather your things. You have a right to do this with dignity and care for the things you value.

Goodbye—and Take Your Stuff

If he's the one moving out, give him the same consideration. He'll need private time to pack and move his stuff. The trick is to accommodate this while being firm about needing him to do this now—not later. But what if he takes off and leaves his stuff behind? This can feel like being "slimed"—left with unpleasant (and perhaps dirty and stinky) reminders of the breakup.

Lonely Street

> Even if he's taken off without his stuff, don't throw it in the trash. If he wants his items later, or just needs an excuse to contact you, you'll be entangled with him all over again. Instead, provide a reasonable timeline to pick up his stuff and *document* that you have done so. Better yet, pack it up, drive it to his new residence, and be done with it.

In this situation, the best you can do is give him notice that you'll be packing his stuff if he doesn't do it himself by a certain date (like yesterday). Yeah, it's a pain, but this is a breakup and pain's a part of it. So the first step is to pack it and either put it out of your way in a storage area or mail it to him. The bright side is that packing him away may help you say goodbye. (Yeah, it's a lame bright side, but we take what we can.)

Yours, Mine, and Ours

As you can see, the bottom line on stuff is (*à la* Larry the Cable Guy): "Git 'r done." If you have mutual stuff, pick your battles. Rules of thumb on shared property are as follows:

- If you brought or bought it, take it. If he did, let it go.

- If it came from your friends or family, it's yours. The same applies to him.

- If you bought it together, decide if it's really important to you. If not, let it go. If so, tell him you would like it. Be a good negotiator by offering up what you know is important to him.

- Even if you hate him, grit your teeth and be fair. Don't give him a reason to be more of a jerk or prolong the relationship. Git 'r done!

What About the Gifts?

Gifts are gifts and, once given, belong to the recipient. The only possible exception to this is an engagement ring (which is coming up). Otherwise, if you want it, you get to keep it, no guilt necessary—gifts are a valid part of your history. But this goes both ways. Your ex deserves to keep what you've given to him, even if it was really expensive and now feel like it was a bad investment.

There are times, however, when you no longer want the gift. Returning, giving away, or pawning a gift may help you symbolically free yourself of the attachment. If your ex sees the item as a tie to you, giving it back will clarify things. Sometimes a gift is not a sign of attachment, but of deceit. In these cases, the gift feels tainted and toxic. For example, if he gave you a string of pearls to appease you while he was sleeping with someone else, you may not only want to return them, but to cut the string and dump them on his floor. But you might want to check if they're real first—living well on a trade-in may be the best revenge!

What About the Ring?

Can you keep the engagement ring? If you break it off, mutually end it, or you sleep with his brother (or sister), hand the bling over.

But what if he breaks off the engagement (or sleeps with *your* sister)? The simple answer is: it depends. Most states punish the jerk and let you keep it. These are "at-fault" states. If you're lucky enough to live in one of these states, the ring may be a lovely consolation prize—especially if sold and applied toward a Club Med trip!

"No-fault" states find at-fault states chauvinistic, and don't want to be bothered with "irrelevant" issues such as who ripped your heart in two and caused it to bleed on the court's expensive new carpet. In these states, you will likely be required to return the ring to the "donor." Check with your lawyer.

Fear Factor

Another challenge of carrying out a breakup is the potential for intimidation or harassment by the ex. Let's look at the ways he might use fear to keep you hooked.

Suicide Threats and Emotional Blackmail

One of the most powerful hooks you can experience after a breakup is the threat of suicide. This is a form of emotional blackmail that says, "You are responsible for what I do to myself." Emotional blackmail can come through exhibits of other self-destructive behaviors such as crying on the phone, binge drinking, drug use, quitting work, staying in bed, or engaging in high-risk activities.

When your ex slimes you with his self-destructiveness, you need to be *very* clear: *you are NOT the one who can help him.* You can tell him to get help, or call 911 and let the cops handle it (they will investigate a suicide threat, and one night in a psychiatric ward may change your ex's tune). Beyond that, make it clear that he cannot call you. If necessary, change your number or block his calls. The more you respond, the more you empower the threats. See threats for what they are: expressions of aggression and anger as well as attempts to control you.

What if the threat feels real? Well, if it didn't you wouldn't be scared. I know the feeling, and I also know what freed me. I told my therapist that I was afraid a man in my life would kill himself because I finally made my boundaries clear. She calmly responded, "If he does, that is his choice." I felt a huge load drop off of my shoulders. Your ex's life is in his hands, not yours. Period.

Read My Lips: Stopping Stalkers

As with emotional blackmail, the best response to harassment is to state and enforce your boundaries. Tell him not to call or come over—no exceptions, end of conversation. Don't talk him about it, because then you are talking! As a general rule, if someone's behavior is not being reinforced, they eventually quit. Make his efforts completely unrewarding by not answering his calls, not answering the door (install a peephole so that you can check before you open), not answering his e-mails—you get the picture.

Meanwhile, document everything so that you're prepared if you need to get a restraining order. Keep a special notebook for this purpose. Write down your communication to him and date it; they'll want to know that you told him not to contact you. Then record every attempt he makes to contact you. E-mails are handy because you can print them off; you can also audio-record phone messages. Beyond protecting you, these efforts will take you out of the victim role and into the role of investigator.

Remember that law enforcement is there to protect citizens like you. Don't hesitate to call for help if you feel scared or just want some advice. A local cop can even make a friendly visit to your ex (in uniform with polished gun) to "suggest" that he stop harassing you.

The Least You Need to Know

- Be clear about what breaking up means.
- Enforce boundaries; don't talk about them.
- Friendship is *not* a good consolation prize.
- Separate your stuff as quickly as possible.
- You are not responsible for your ex's response to the break up, but you are responsible for protecting yourself.

The Endless "Why?"

In This Chapter

- Stuck on "Why?"
- Getting past it
- What you *can* control
- Allowing adventure

When you're the one who broke things off, you've pretty much got "Why?" figured out. But if you got the shaft, you have some catching up to do. You need to get into your ex's head and figure out what went wrong. Or do you?

This chapter will look at the temptation to focus on your ex after being dumped. We naturally want to know and understand, and we probably have already gotten some parting feedback. Maybe we sensed or even fought about problems before the breakup occurred. If we reflect a minute, we can usually get in touch with the part of us that knows the answer. But the Post-Breakup Why is about more than knowing.

We'll look at these hidden motives and traps, and reveal the Why for what it is. We'll also identify the bad answers that we can arrive at in responding to Why. Once we've loosened the grip of Why, we'll shift the focus to you and what you want, and get ready for what's next.

If you're spinning around and around with the same questions, feeling immobilized, and waiting for something that's not happening, then read on. This chapter will help you stop the spinning and start the adventure.

The "Why?" Trap

After getting dumped, we want answers! We want the truth! We want *The Answer*. Once equipped with this wisdom, we will say, "Ah!" then smile and quickly move on.

Nice theory. "Why" is one of the biggest, craftiest, and most effective traps we can fall into after a breakup. The Why question offers the promise of insight while keeping us in the very same place we started.

It helps to think of Why as a devil in therapist's clothing, tempting us to keep asking questions we don't want the answer to or will not accept the answer to. Let's use an example: Say you've been dumped. You ask your ex, "Why?" He says, "I loved you, but wasn't *in* love with you." Are you going to say, "Oh, *that's* it! Well, thank you. Now I understand. Have a wonderful life"?

Lonely Street

> Drunk-dialing the ex after too much Jägermeister? Big mistake! The booze goes right to your heart and floods the Whys and longings over the rim. Grabbing the phone through an alcoholic haze is your addled brain trying to fix the heartache. *STOP! This will make things worse.* If you really want to "talk," call your most understanding girlfriend—or just go to bed. Going to bed would be good. Bed. Go there.

More likely, you're going to wonder, "What is that supposed to mean? How can you not be *in love* with me? What happened?" And so on.

In this example, the Why is a statement of protest, not a true question. Think about it: is there any answer that will make it all right? Yet, the Why-Devil convinces us that if we ask enough times, we might get an answer we like.

Another tactic of the Why-Devil is to convince us that an explanation will take away the pain, or protect us from pain in the future. Sure, it sounds good to say, "I'll figure out the mistake and never make it again, and then I'll never get hurt again."

The problem is, what you decide is a mistake may be one of your best qualities. For example, maybe you're really funny in groups, and your ex felt overshadowed by you. You can either decide that his insecurity is his problem, or conclude that your funny side is a problem that needs correcting. The latter conclusion may satisfy the Why-Devil, but leaves you deprived of a really cool part of yourself—and something the next guy might find irresistible! Don't you dare give it up!

Why It Happened: Bad Answers

As the previous example reveals, we often trash ourselves as a way of explaining things. Alternatively, we might trash the outside world. After all, better to blame than to admit we've been hurt. While giving us a false sense of control, these "answers" do far more damage than any breakup could.

Nobody Loves Me

Deciding you are unlovable simplifies things. You can collect examples of other times you were rejected, and make a case for being unable to attract love in the future. Of course, you're ignoring many examples of being loved and wanted, but that would complicate things. The Why-Devil likes things very simple.

So let's make a mess for the Why-Devil. If you're tempted to conclude that nobody loves you, start a list of everyone who does love you. Even if you can only think of God and your dog, it's a start. Then write down everything Spot loves so much about you, what your mama and your best friend see in you, why your mailman seems to linger when he delivers your mail, everything that contradicts the easy way out. Keep the list handy and add to it as more examples come to mind.

Nobody's Worth Loving

"Nobody's worth loving" is another easy explanation that the Why-Devil promotes. Related conclusions include "All men are jerks," "All the good ones are taken," and "They'll all hurt you in the end." These me-against-the-world positions can feel safe and cozy for a while, giving you good reason not to risk your heart again. But, like a little girl during a pouting session, you start to get lonely and secretly wish someone would come and knock on the door. Again, a messy world full of possibilities is better than the simple one the Why-Devil tries to sell.

So, mess it up! Begin a new list of people in your life who are worthy of your love. Then add all the pleasures that come with loving them, from buying the just-right gift to knowing the intimate secrets of their lives. Allow yourself to embrace the world—it's rich with lovers as well as jerks!

Should Have Known

Of the simplified explanations the Why-Devil promotes, "I should have known" is the most overused of them all. Here's how it goes: "I should have known" things wouldn't work out; he would cheat; he was an experienced con man. And "If I had known," I would have gotten out and saved myself all this grief. Therefore, even if he was the lowest scum of the earth, *it was all my fault!*

Lovely. And it gets worse. If you buy into, "I should have known," you get the bonus of, *"I'll know in the future."* Therefore, you'll never date anyone without a 100 percent guarantee that nothing will go wrong. In other words, you just don't date.

 Breakup Repair

> We ask "Why?" to recover a sense of control. Apply that energy to something constructive: sort the papers on your desk, the junk in your drawers—even take on the closet. Sorting and clearing space is a great way to assert control over your life. You get to toss what you don't want, keep what you like, and put it where you want. Treat yourself to attractive storage containers, dividers for drawers, or sachets for your closet. Enjoy!

One of the assumptions of "I should have known" is that the relationship should not have happened, that only pain-free experiences are of value. Even the worst relationships usually have something to offer us, though it may take awhile to figure out what it was! And we usually can't tell if we've found a prince until we've kissed the toad. I'd say it's better to kiss a few extra toads if it means landing a prince—not to mention the royal jewels and the real estate!

When "Why?" Is Worth Asking

If you seem stuck in a story that keeps repeating itself, "Why?" may be an important question. A helpful rule of thumb is, when it's a pattern, you're probably doing something to keep it going. In the case of being dumped, you could be (a) Doing something to drive men away, or (b) Selecting men who leave. Let's look at both possibilities.

The "Leave Me" Story

While you're not consciously telling guys to leave you, you may be putting out signals that you're expecting to be left. For example, if you're dancing around trying to please him, he may read through the lines that you don't expect much from him, or that maybe you don't even expect him to hang around. Another version of this story would be that you're so into pleasing him that he doesn't even see or know who *you* actually are. How can he have the chance to love you?

The "Leave me" message can come through almost any behavior, from combativeness (maybe your dad was a bully and that's what you expect from him) to clinginess (you feel you have to hold on or else he'll leave). Take care here, though. There's a difference between having your own personality and having a self-destructive pattern. You may be more dependent than your girlfriends and still be emotionally healthy. That's called personality, and it's one of the things that make you uniquely loveable. If you have an unhealthy pattern, you're repeating old pain in the present. If this is what's happening, give yourself the gift of a good therapist and leave the pain behind.

The Bad Choice Story

Maybe your pattern is to pick guys who leave. You're not alone. There can be something attractive about the aloof bad-boy who stays with you long enough to melt your heart and then moves on. If you're a player, too, maybe the joke's on him. But usually we want more—maybe we can be the one to reform him! *Please*.

But don't be too hard on yourself. These guys are good at what they do, and sometimes the performance is worth it. But you have a right to expect more. You can have sexy and loyal, confident and caring. If you're not convinced of that, get some help in building your sense of worth. And remember, in the words of Mae West, "Too much of a good thing is wonderful!"

From "Why?" to "What Now?"

Perhaps, the biggest problem with Why, is that it gets focused on events and people we can't control. Here's the Why-Devil's genius at work: "Why" keeps you focused on—maybe even obsessed with—your ex's motives, needs, and goals. Meanwhile, you completely forget about what *you* need and want!

Try shifting your focus from "Why did he leave?" to "What do I want?" Okay, so the answer might be, "My ex." But is that true? Do you want everything about him, including what led him to break up with you? Okay, so maybe you want everything but the breakup part. That's cool. But since you've already modified him, you might as well think about what else you might change. Perhaps you'd like a better listener? Someone more successful? Better endowed?

Notice how you suddenly feel less desperate when you put yourself in the position of evaluator? It's a simple shift, but an extremely powerful one. You move from being a nervous contestant on *American Idol* to being a judge—maybe Paula Abdul rather than Simon Cowell, but still, your place on the show is secure.

You always have the power to choose, whether you identify your preferences right now or when you view the "contestants" in your life.

Blazing New Trails

So, what happens when you let go and leave all your "Why"s in the dust? You'll probably feel a bit uneasy—lighter, but also less grounded. You have entered uncharted territory. If you're feeling shaky and vulnerable, congratulate yourself! You are no longer comfortably stuck, looking to someone else for cues on living your life. Moving on without assumptions or instructions is exciting as well as scary, but that's the definition of adventure. You could meet almost *anyone* in this new place.

But there is some extremely helpful equipment you can bring with you. You'll need your knowledge of yourself, of what works for you and what doesn't. This will protect you from getting detoured by a crummy relationship and will help you notice when you're on the right track. Take your shopping skills: browse a lot of options before making choices, notice what you like, and admit what looks bad on you. And bring your dreams, because, in a world that's beyond your control, *anything can happen.* Sometimes all you need is to be ready.

There will be challenges, of course. Emptiness is a natural part of transition. Relax—it's only temporary. You'll have days when you feel lonely and tired and long for your old life, even if it was miserable! The Why-Devil may try to pull you back, but just keep walking. You don't have to feel brave and strong—and chances are you won't for awhile—but it's what we *do* that defines courage, not how we feel. Surviving a breakup is an accomplishment—getting past Why is worthy of a medal!

Finding Travel Partners

Never underestimate the power of girlfriends to help you get through the hardest parts of the journey. If you don't have girlfriends around for support, you're not alone. When you've been deep into a relationship, it's easy to neglect friendships.

First of all, learn your lesson once and for all: your friends are important, whether you're dating or not. From now on, *never* cancel out on your girlfriends to go out on a date!

Contact the friends you've neglected and make amends. If you're not that close with anyone, list the friends and acquaintances you'd like to spend more time with, and pick three to invite to lunch. If you know of somebody who's recently gone through a breakup, you'll have an instant connection! Call or e-mail your top picks for the week—it'll take some time to connect and work out your schedules.

To meet new friends, sign up for a class you've been wanting to take. I got a whole new pack of like-minded girlfriends by signing up for a class in memoir writing. You've probably heard the "take-a-class" advice for meeting dates as well. The logic is the same—you find people you like by doing things you like—but the approach seems to work better for finding girlfriends. After all, women are the ones who sign up for self-help gigs (*obviously*), take courses in creative expression, and seek social support at times of crisis. It's not that guys aren't capable of this, but there still tends to be a stigma. (You should have seen the female-to-male ratio at my last book tour!)

You're actually at a very good time to establish lasting friendships. The old saying, "A friend in need is a friend indeed," still holds: we bond most deeply at times of vulnerability. So before you even *think* about finding another boyfriend, get some girlfriends! Take them on your journey and you'll not only travel lighter, but you'll have way more fun!

The Least You Need to Know

- We use "Why" to try to change what happened or regain control.
- Although we think it offers progress, "Why" keeps us stuck.
- Answers to "Why" can be self-destructive; "What do I want?" is a better question.
- Focus on friendships now; leave romance for later.

Awkward Epilogues

In This Chapter

- Being haunted by the ex
- Brain damage that comes with temptation
- Avoiding setbacks
- Letting go of the ex's community
- Dealing with your friends and family

Even after you've closed the door on the relationship—and perhaps locked and bolted it—and even after you've given up the "Why?" and started to focus on your own life, your ex may haunt you. No, he won't show up as a transparent apparition, but as a thought, a wish, a regret. These hauntings usually have a trigger, whether it is an association (smelling his favorite cologne), a direct reminder (hearing someone talk about him), or a live sighting (he's shopping across from you in the produce section).

Fallout from the breakup may also haunt you. You might feel uncomfortable with mutual friends, or if your family was attached to him, they might be pining or acting weird themselves. And the worst sightings are the ones that include the ex's new girl-friend. Now that's just frightening!

Whatever the trigger, there are going to be times when you'll suddenly be slapped in the face with everything you thought you'd left behind: old feelings, wishes, desires, regrets, and, yes, the endless "Why?"

When this happens, you're at risk for some serious brain damage; the kind that threatens to wipe out all your progress and send you directly back to square one. In this chapter, we'll discuss the types of hauntings you may encounter, the temporary brain damage that occurs, and how you can counter its effects and get on with your life.

Post-Breakup Temptations

So you're out with your friends: the band is hot, you're in a great mood, and you know you look good. You've even gotten over *him*. That is until you *see* him across the room, looking as good as you do. Worse, he flashes that smile at you. Your heart starts pumping and, suddenly, he is the only person in the room.

Your friends move to Red Alert, slapping your cheeks and reminding you what that cute guy did to you. But all you can do is mumble under your breath, "But he looks sooo good." You free yourself from their grip and, like a patient under the trance of a hypnotist, you move toward that smile.

Breakup Repair

When you're tempted to start something with your ex, it helps to think of the craving as part of an addiction. Cravings are to be expected, but indulging them only strengthens the addiction. Cold turkey is the most effective route to healing. While indulging gives you temporary relief, standing firm in the face of cravings gives you a different kind of satisfaction—the power to control your cravings rather than let them control you.

Sound familiar? If so, you know that this is just the beginning of the brain damage you suffer in the face of post-breakup temptation.

Talk It Out

To continue our saga: As you walk toward him, your mind is racing with thoughts like, "Maybe if we just talked it out, maybe things weren't all that bad, maybe we could start over …."

Maybe. Maybe not. Your brain is not only suffering from tunnel vision—dissing your friends and your newly found self-esteem—but also from amnesia. Seeing the dressed-up version of him takes you back to a time before you knew better. Suddenly all those old hopes, desires, and expectations fill your system like a toxic gas. You forget that ...

- He treated you like crap.
- You've "talked it out" about a hundred million times.
- You needed antidepressants to put up with him.
- He can be embarrassingly stupid.

No, now he's perfect, everything you dreamed of.

Wake up! What talking it out will do (unless he—or both of you—has put at least a year of therapy under his belt) will prolong the misery that you worked like hell to get out of. You'll get everything stirred up again, you'll probably fight, and you'll end up feeling like crap. *Again.* And after all the progress you've made!

However, the reality is, you may need to do it. We're human, and sometimes we just need to hit our heads against the wall a few times to be sure that it really hurts. So, if you do it, don't beat yourself up; just *learn.* Beating yourself up is a sneaky part of the brain damage: it's a part of what keeps you tied up in the past.

You won't lose the gains you made if you just get back on track. Apologize (again) to your friends, apologize to yourself—and *forgive* yourself—then pick up where you left off. Congratulate yourself for letting go—again!

Sleepover

Let's say that, instead of hoping to save the relationship, you're just honest with yourself and say, "I know it won't work between us, but he looks good and I deserve a little love." You convince yourself that a little sleepover won't do any harm.

Yeah, right. Brain-damage alert! If all you want is a romp, you'd be better off hiring Deuce Bigalow. Although the brain damage is restricted to the area of sex rather than the whole love-and-marriage package, it is still causing you to forget …

- All the work you've done to try to forget him.
- The fact that you'll have to say goodbye *all over again!*
- How pissed your girlfriends will be at you.
- How pissed YOU will be at you.
- That you have a heart and it can be broken (again).
- The increased cost of therapy and antidepressants.

So what do you do when the temptations arise? First of all, remind yourself that you are suffering from temporary brain damage. Then help your brain compensate. For example, if he looks good, pull out the grossest picture of him from your memory, or invent one. Think of him scratching his butt, or put a big zit on the tip of his nose. If he's being charming, remember the nastiest thing he said to you and put it in an imaginary cartoon bubble above his head. If he seems open to reform, see him as a sleaze machine trying to conquer you for kicks. If it helps, picture him with a gold medallion, fake fur, and a pimped-out Caddy!

If all this seems harsh, think of all the harshness you are saving yourself and get out! Once you are securely away from him and your brain begins to recover, reward yourself big time. Call all your friends and let them congratulate you, book yourself a massage *and* a pedicure, and bask in your own courage and strength.

Separation Implications

The ripple effect of a breakup can catch us by surprise. If you were in your relationship for a long time, people in your world probably got used to seeing you as a couple. Unless your friends and family hated your ex from the start and are singing your praises right now, they're probably feeling the breakup and the loss as well. There are people who became part of your life through your ex, and you may be missing them. In fact, there are times we learn that the people in your ex's world are harder to let go of than the ex!

Friends

First, let's talk about the friends who were yours before there was an "us." How did things change when you got serious with your ex? Did they feel abandoned or happy for you? Did they enjoy being with the two of you? Did their worlds expand along with yours? Are they "couples" as well?

Your friends may be happy to have you back, mad you were gone, sad to lose your ex, or guilty because you're not in a couple right now and they are. Most likely, you're experiencing different responses from different friends. And, as we discussed in Chapter 4, you may find yourself detached from previous or single friends because you blew them off for a lover. Thankfully, girlfriends are usually pretty resilient to changes in boyfriend status. They know how it is and have probably done the same. But you still may have some repair to do.

It can be particularly hard to face a friend who saw problems in the relationship before you were willing to admit them. You may have even lost a friend over the conflict. If you're not eager to go to her and say, "You were right and I was wrong," join the club. It's hard to do a 180 and put yourself on the side of a former adversary. But remember, unless she's a sadist, it is usually very hard for a friend to tell you that you're making a bad decision. To be fair to both of you, admit that she saw something you weren't ready to see, but you needed to find out for yourself. You can thank her for caring and for her courage to be honest. If you were hard on her before, apologize.

What about the couple pairs and new friends you made through your ex? This can be tricky territory, and there will be some fallout. No one can sit on the fence forever: sooner or later your mutual friends will hang with one of you or the other. As a rule of thumb, the friends you came with are yours, and the friends he came with are his. Occasionally, if one of you was a total jerk, a friend may jump ship and join the other crew. But don't expect this. Old loyalties run deep, and a part of friendship is sticking around even when you've been a jerk. See how valuable friends are?

Lonely Street

Watch for friends who find it irresistible to report to you on the ex's activities. They're probably not doing it to be mean; they're just attached to the drama. Here's where you need to be *very* clear: you don't want any "ex reports." For extra credit, ask them to stop *you* if you talk about him. As tempting as the drama is, you're not in the audience and you can get hurt. If you want drama, rent a movie!

But losing his friends can make adjusting to a breakup harder. Keep in mind that it's probably difficult for them as well. Like kids caught in a divorce, they may be unsettled by it all. Try not to blame them or take their loyalties personally.

Friends of yours who are also in couples may feel awkward about sharing their good feelings about their relationships. Although this may be hard for you, too, try to see it as evidence that love is possible and can happen for you. However, the reality is that you may have less in common right now—you want to go look for guys and she just wants to be with hers. Regardless of what the concerns are, if the friendship is important to you, put it on the table and talk! Share your worries and fears. Some of them may only be in your head!

Family

Ah, family. Let's face it, most families are weird, so they'll probably have some weird ways of dealing with the breakup. They may treat you like a porcelain doll, giving you a look of pity every time they see you. Maybe they'll express "concern" that you were too hard on him, or develop strategies for how to get you back together. They might even try to set you up with that nice, perpetually single guy from back home.

Whatever their response, try to see the humor in it. Step back and appreciate the quirkiness of their responses; watch it like a movie rather than taking it in. Sure it feels crummy to be treated like an invalid or a leper because you're suddenly single, but if you focus on their behavior, it's the kind of material that makes for good comedy (think *My Big Fat Greek Wedding*)!

Every family is like an itty bitty country with its own culture and language. Your family's language for showing they care may be pretty limited. Try not to confuse these limitations for criticism. Accept the intent behind it and move on. (And you get to decide how much time you want to spend in the "old country.")

Then there's *his* family. Often, when we are attracted to someone, we're also attracted to the family he comes from. This attraction can be there before we even meet them. We tend to be drawn to families that offer something our own families don't. This is why it can be hard to separate from the ex's family. If your family culture emphasized distance and a businesslike attitude, you may have fed off of his family's hugs and warmth. Sometimes we discover that the attraction to the ex was *more* about his family than him! This is a great clue to what we need to build into our lives, but not a good reason to stay with someone who's not a match.

You can write a letter to say thanks and goodbye to the ex's family, but *do not* mention the ex. You will only stir up bad feelings. It does hurt to think that their view of you may have changed, but you'll only make it worse if you tell them what a lousy son they produced!

Awkward Encounters

It's one thing to see your ex across the room when you're dressed up and feeling great, but encounters usually don't happen so elegantly. Let's talk about how to keep yourself together when you bump into him—or worse, him and his new girlfriend.

Running Into the Ex

Depending on the relationship you had and who did the dumping, an accidental encounter will arouse any number of feelings—all in a split second. We've all had those situations that render us speechless until we finally come up with the right thing to say—two days later!

Well, clever lines only work in the movies, anyway. Let's play worst-case scenario. Think about what response will keep you out of disaster's way:

1. *The arrogant jerk who cheated on you sees you on a bad-hair day in your dumpiest sweats, complete with extra sweat!* **Feelings:** Embarrassment, regret, anger.

2. *The sweet guy you dumped sees you with another guy.* **Feelings:** Guilt, sadness, pity, more guilt.

3. *The love of your life is at the drugstore counter buying condoms as the pharmacist calls your name and asks you a question about your Prozac dose.* **Feelings:** Humiliation, heart-breaking sadness, anger.

What did you do in case #1? Did you use your running shoes to sprint out of sight? Did you try to fluff your hair and act aloof? Believe me, the aloof act never works. The more you try, the more likely you are to trip on your laces and fall on your face. Better to look him in the eye, say, "Excuse me," and walk on by. Even if you're typically Miss Sunshine, feel free to look unhappy to see him. Rule of thumb is this: don't waste your emotions on him.

Okay now, what about the sweet guy you left? Do you act friendly and introduce him to your new friend? Do you try to avoid eye contact? Here's where the Golden Rule helps: don't you dare treat him with pity or exaggerated friendliness! You can acknowledge him with a look, enabling him to maintain his privacy. If he says "Hi," say "Hi" back. Move on. He's a big boy.

Breakup Repair

One trick to handling awkward moments is to *let them to be awkward.* This is a shift for a lot of us—women are accustomed to filling in uncomfortable moments. We smile to cover negative feelings; we babble to fill in the silence. Although these efforts can make *others* more comfortable, they often undermine our own strength. There is power in truth, even when the truth is as simple as withholding a smile.

Now for the hardest one: the love-of-your-life ex. While it's not likely you'll enact the scenario, how would you respond? Again, cover-ups only make things worse. Let the moment pass, but save the story. Think David Sedaris or Bridget Jones: when you're doing the telling, a story like this makes you comedic and loveable.

As these scenarios reveal, an ounce of honest acknowledgment is usually all that's needed. But the "ounce" part is crucial: no spilling your guts, no hanging around. Often a look or a nod is sufficient.

The Ex's New Squeeze

Okay, here is the *worst* worst-case scenario: you're walking along by yourself (for effect, add bad hair and Saturday night), and you encounter your ex and his too-attractive girlfriend, arm in arm, teasing and loving on each other. Of course, you *want* to disappear, but it's too late. They see you.

As with other awkward encounters, you don't need to put out a lot of effort. Acknowledge him and walk on by. Hopefully, he won't have time to introduce her, but if he does, say a simple "Hey" and then move on like you've gotta be somewhere—anywhere!

This is a haunting of the worst kind, and unless you are way over him, you will feel just about every emotion in the book: humiliation, betrayal, sadness, rage, envy, competition, did I mention rage?

Seeing your ex looking happy in a relationship is very distressing. As a friend of mine put it, "I'm angry *he* gets the happy ending!" But, after more thought, the same friend said, "He's still the same guy. He's only able to give her what he gave me."

If you are haunted by how well your ex is living, it's easy to put energy into the wish for him to fall on his face. But wait a minute: your focus just went back to *him*, and away from you. You are spending energy on him, not you. Yet, this energy has absolutely no effect on him, and it hurts you. Rotten deal, huh? As Nelson Mandela put it, "Resentment is like drinking poison and waiting for it to kill your enemy."

So when you are haunted, drive him out, not by fighting the thoughts, but by shifting them to your own life. Make your own desires and interests so big that there isn't room for your ex. Exorcise the ex! And when you get to the point where you render him invisible, you have accomplished the best revenge: you have eliminated him.

The Least You Need to Know

- Talking it out won't go any better the second, or third, or fourth time.
- Sex is more than sex.
- Family and friends may be grieving, too.
- Allow your ex's friends and family to be loyal to him.
- Focus on your life, not his.

Chapter 6

It's Over (Again): Serial Breakups

In This Chapter

- When breaking up becomes a habit
- Breakup-makeup payoffs
- Breakup-makeup costs
- The quest for resolution
- Alternatives to fight-or-flight

Like any good story, a romance is more interesting when a crisis threatens its happy resolution. At least that's the way it works in the movies. Watch almost any romantic comedy, and some misunderstanding, temptation, or conflict of values sends someone away crying or swearing, and every possible obstacle comes in the way of clearing things up. Then, just as the chances for reconciliation are about to run out (often due to an airplane's departure), the power of love overcomes the obstacles, the lovers meet up and breathlessly confess their true feelings.

The tension caused by the crisis makes the movie's ending all the sweeter. We get to cry, feel the love, and see the world as a beautiful place again. Sometimes the drama captivates us so much that we go back and see the movie over and over again.

Some of us, however, *live* the drama, over and over, through serial breakups (and makeups) with the same person. Participants in the real version become hooked on the intensity of fighting and reuniting, welcome the opportunities to express passionate feeling, and seize the power of dramatic exits and entrances.

House lights! Let's step back from the drama and take time for a critical review.

The Breakup-Makeup Drama

Ever noticed how, when you're in a serial-breakup cycle, you become captivated by the drama? In fact, it's just about all you think about—and talk about. Meanwhile, your friends and family are bored to tears. In fact, a sure sign that you are stuck in a neurosis—a form of repetitive, self-inflicted suffering—is that the story is *boring*. Rather than facing real loss or reconciliation, you stay—perhaps miserably, yet comfortably, undecided.

Breakup Bytes

As a relationship becomes more serious and the two of you begin to spend more time together, conflicts often arise. For example, if one of you enjoys the party life and the other does not drink, the difference can become more challenging. It is not uncommon for a couple to reach a **breaking point**—a point of tension that either breaks or strengthens the pair's resolve to be together. When the desire for each other is strong enough, and the conflict does not break you apart, the real "ending" (which is actually a beginning) can feel as powerful as a movie reel's ending.

Here are some other differences between "reel life" and real life breakup-makeup (BUMU) dramas:

Reel Life	Real Life
BUMU proves power of love	BUMUs reveal weak relationship
BUMU enhances drama	BUMUs eliminate risk
BU often due to silly mix-up	BUs often due to value conflict
Conflict overcome by love	Conflict avoided by BUMU cycle

Just as with real-life serial breakups, romantic comedies often miss the ongoing challenge of conflict. (For an exception, see *The Story of Us*. It's not a comedy.) At the end of the movie, as the couple walks off into the sunset or teasingly feed each other wedding cake, we imagine that all is forgiven and the rest is, well, cake. We don't want to see the fight re-emerge in a different context. This may be why we often feel overwhelmed when conflicts do resurface—and they usually do! We forget that there is a third alternative to breaking up or imposing a false happy ending—it's called *working it out*.

Playing the Breakup Card

You don't have to be a drama queen to get hooked on serial breakups. Breaking up can be a way of communicating or even an attempt to improve the relationship. Let's look at some common reasons people pull out the breakup card.

For Control

Maybe you really like the guy you're with, but you're fed up with something he's doing. You tell him, and he gets defensive or points the finger back at you. No matter what you try, you can't seem to get through to him. You're tired of not being taken seriously, so you get serious. You tell him you're through and walk out.

But ... you may walk slowly, secretly hoping he'll catch up. You don't want to end the relationship;

you want leverage. You want to raise the stakes so that he'll pay attention. You've put up with his neglect too long and now he'll need to work a little harder to get back what he had.

Lonely Street

> Before you break up for a purpose other than breaking up, consider whether this is the way you want your relationship to work. Do you want to have to leave to be heard? How do you feel about yourself when you have to go to such lengths? If you've been left, do you really want to beg back in? We all have fantasies about others appreciating us more when we're gone, but in reality, being appreciated while we're there is a much better deal.

Of course, the plan may backfire: he calls your bluff and lets you go. Then you have to decide whether to stick with the exit or come running back with even less power.

But then, sometimes the breakup card works. He reflects on what happened and puts in that extra effort to win you back. You regain the power you were lacking. You're thinking, "Hmm, that play might come in handy another time …."

For Change

When you hit up against a deal-breaker in a relationship, but you don't want to lose the good stuff, what do you do? Well, you could make a tough choice between your principles and the relationship, try to work it through together, or you could pull out the breakup card. This kind of breakup comes with a subtle ultimatum: "If you change the unacceptable part of you, I'll come back."

Let's say, for example, that your partner is drinking too much. You're beginning to worry that he's an alcoholic, and there's no way you can live with that. But otherwise he's great! So all you need for him to do is change the drinking part and everything will be perfect. So you say adios, and tell him to call you when he's got a handle on his drinking.

Here's what often happens in relationships dependent on serial breakups: he calls a week later, and says he's not drinking. You run into his open arms. Then you toast the occasion (one drink won't hurt). Somehow, the booze starts trickling back into his life. Eventually, you leave (again), and so on.

Although this example is more obvious than life usually is, the pattern is the same. The payoff? You get to hold on to your principles and he gets to hold on to the booze.

For the Makeup

If you're really going for the movie moment, you might call it quits just for the possibility of that sweet reconciliation. Through serial breakups, you get to begin the relationship over and over, keeping things exciting and new.

Like any addiction, though, the high of the makeup comes at a greater and greater cost. The rest of the time, you know you're not really getting what you want and you're closing the door on other opportunities. But just when you decide this is really it—you're not going back, he shows up with a bouquet of handpicked flowers and that look in his eyes, and you're under the addiction's spell.

The Cost of Repetition

It may seem like serial breakups solve a lot of problems—you keep things fresh, check out when things get hard—but the "solution" comes at an increasingly high price. First of all, rejection still hurts, whether you suspect it's temporary or not. Second, the relationship never really feels secure, even when it's "on." Despite the temporary gratification, you carry around the awareness that things really aren't any better, and that starts to wear away at your sense of competence. On top of it all, you have to sheepishly tell your friends, "Well, I gave him one more chance," while they roll their eyes and remind you that you said that the last time.

Breakup Repair

If you're getting down on yourself for your history of serial breakups, STOP! There wouldn't be a chapter on the topic if it weren't a common problem. Nobody likes being stuck in a pattern that isn't getting you anywhere. Yet, in reality, repetition is often necessary for you to ultimately see things as they are. After the third time that he swears he's stopped drinking and later reeks of alcohol, you learn. Allow yourself the benefit of time served and move on.

But what we really minimize is what serial breakups do to the relationship. Let's explore these costs next.

Losing Credibility

Just as a known bluffer loses her effectiveness at the poker table, overusing the breakup card gives you less credibility with your partner. The irony is that the breakup threats and dramatic exits come out of a desire to be taken seriously, yet the effect is the opposite. Sadly, the most effective exits are the permanent ones. How many times have you seen a friend tell her boyfriend exactly what she needs, only to have him miffed (but finally curious) when she leaves? But think about it: if someone is so dense that it takes leaving to get his attention, do you really want him anyway?

Losing Trust

After someone has run out on you, it's simply harder to feel safe in the relationship. Questions may linger in the back of your mind. Is it okay to disagree? If you make a mistake, will there be time to work it out? Being left hurts, and the hurt leaves an impression. This is a reality often neglected in the movies, where the love confession supposedly cures—and erases—everything.

When partners lose trust in each other, they start to keep a part of themselves out of the relationship. Rather than dealing with sensitive issues, they might hold back and even lie to keep things going smoothly. Alternatively, old hurts can resurface and come up in unexpected places. For example, an argument about one of you being late for the concert might turn into a fight about the time one of you didn't show up at all.

Losing the Relationship

The most obvious risk of breaking up when you don't really want to is that your partner might accept your decision. Maybe he doesn't really want to run after you, especially after you just rejected him. Or maybe he's crazy about you, but his pride keeps him from acting.

Bottom line? If you don't want to break up, don't. Get in there and work it out. Or if trying gets you nowhere, hang around until you get the courage to really say goodbye, and then say goodbye. And when you break up for real, you can take along your integrity, your self-respect, and your trust that the world has more in store for you.

 Breakup Bytes

> Not your typical romantic comedy, *The Break-Up*, starring Jennifer Aniston and Vince Vaughn, reveals the dark side of breaking up as relationship strategy. The warfare between the exes makes up the comic element, as captured in Gary's (Vaughn) retort: "Is that how you want to play it, Brooke? Because I can play it like that. I can play it like Lionel Richie: *All Night Long*." At the same time, their vulnerability and the consequences of the breakup give more meat to the flick. The movie reveals that breaking up is a powerful play, but its power doesn't only affect the one being played.

Fight, Flight or Insight?

When conflict occurs, we get stressed. When we get stressed, we instinctively want to fight or flee, and this is what fuels serial breakups. Some of us are fighters, eager to get in there and verbally duke it out until there's a resolution. Some of us are repelled by conflict, and prefer to flee the scene and wait for things to cool off.

In the case of serial breakups, fight and flight control the relationship. The fighter scares away the flyer, and the flyer subdues the fighter. Or two fighters push to win rather than resolve. Two flyers don't even show for the fight. Yet the hope of resolution keeps both players in the game. The solution always seems just ahead, tempting the two to stay in a game that they can't play together.

Fortunately, humans have evolved beyond the level of instinct, and we *can* do better. We can fight in a whole new way—for the *relationship*. We can stop fighting and fleeing and look for the real source of the problem. Or we can accept the other person as-is and decide from there. Let's explore these alternatives.

The Good Fight

When you think of a fight, you may imagine physical confrontation or verbal yelling. Either way, two people are attacking each other, hurling punches, insults, accusations, or defensive jabs. When a fight is more like a debate, things may be calmer, but each party is striving to win.

Contrast this with fighting for the relationship. When the desired outcome is a better relationship, the two of you are no longer fighting against each other. Instead, you are fighting for more, with the understanding that getting what you each want will help you feel better about each other. Your thinking shifts from either-or to both-and. Because good fighting goes against instincts, it is a skill worth developing. Check out Appendix D for a crash course.

Insight

Ah, insight. It's often where you turn when all else fails. In the case of serial breakups, there's good reason to look for insight sooner rather than later.

This is because what hooks you into a failing relationship is often something you struggle with in other areas of your life. For example, if you choose a neglectful partner and then break up and make up over his level of attention, neglect may be a theme for you. Perhaps you were a neglected member of your family, and maybe you tend to neglect yourself. When you can identify the theme of your BUMU cycle, you can stop fighting your partner and start fighting the problem.

If Neglect is the enemy, rather than your partner, you can start to pay attention to what the real enemy tells you. Maybe Neglect tells you that you don't really need a present on your birthday. So when your boyfriend asks what you want for your birthday, you say, "I don't really need anything." He doesn't realize that Neglect is speaking (okay, he's a little dense) and takes you literally. On your birthday, you feel heartbroken that he didn't get you anything and you want to yell at him or run away.

One woman I worked with identified her problem as Pressure. She felt pressure from her mother, from her partner, and in social settings. She had nightmares in which she was trapped in bed with a powerful force pushing on her chest, keeping her immobilized, and making it hard for her to breathe. Once she identified Pressure as the problem, she realized that she didn't have to follow Pressure's instructions. As she listened to breakup songs on the radio, they all seemed to be mirroring her feelings about Pressure. So she created a double CD mix of these songs as her tribute to her breakup with Pressure. She did not break up with her partner. Once Pressure was out of the way, the two of them started having fun again.

To get to this kind of insight, take the following steps:

1. Write a list of all the things your partner has done to make you mad.

2. Notice the similarities between the items on the list.

3. Give a name to the problem, such as Judgment, Criticism, Perfectionism, or Betrayal.

4. Listen for the way the problem talks to you.

5. Write a letter to the problem and assert your position.

6. Fight the problem, not the person.

It's important to note that your relationship may be a match made by the problem. In other words, the way your partner talks to you may sound just like the way the problem talks to you. Like a lullaby you heard a million times, the voice is familiar and it hooks you. So the relationship can become a workshop for you to identify and overcome the problem. Once you no longer need the problem, you may no longer want the relationship.

Acceptance

Another very simple way to end a BUMU cycle is to accept your partner. Please note that acceptance does not necessarily mean staying together. Acceptance means saying, "He is doing the best he can and he loves me the best he knows how." This is usually true. How people treat you says much more about them than about you. Now, you may follow the acceptance with a decision to leave the relationship, because his best may not be enough for you. But when you break up this way, you release your partner without resentment or bitterness. This is a far cry from believing that your partner can easily change but just won't.

The Least You Need to Know

- Serial breakups feel dramatic but are actually boring.
- Sometimes people break up to gain power or promote change.
- Breaking up hurts the relationship, even when followed by reconciliation.
- Self-protective instincts contribute to serial breakups.
- When you separate the problem from your partner, you can free yourself from the breakup-makeup cycle.

Chapter 7

Stuck-in-the-Blues Clues

In This Chapter

- Identifying the signs of depression
- Getting help
- Meeting the challenge of emptiness
- How "can't stand" leads to bad solutions
- Acting smart

When we feel bad, it's easy to become overwhelmed and defeated. We forget how we coped in the past, forget that we ever felt good, and can't imagine feeling good again. These are the times when we need a window out of ourselves. We need to see that there is more than what we're stuck in right now.

Once we see out, we can start to work our way to the door and out into the fresh air. This chapter is your window. We'll start by defining what's gotten you stuck, and then look at how you can get out.

As you go through this chapter, watch the temptation to move backward rather than forward. Moving backward happens when we regret, blame ourselves, "should" on ourselves, and think about what we could have done. Moving forward feels weird and awkward, and sometimes scary, but is a lot lighter and more interesting.

Now, this advice can be tricky: if you do move backward, you might want to beat yourself up for that. Don't. Just leave "backward" behind and move forward when you can.

Signs of Depression

Maybe you've tried everything we've talked about but you still feel like someone hit you in the head. You can't seem to perk up and you don't feel like doing anything. Maybe you're sleeping all the time; maybe you can't sleep. You've lost your appetite—or you're eating everything in sight. Even when you get a lot of sleep, you feel tired, and slow, and just "blah."

On top of all of this, your emotional range stretches all the way from guilt to worthlessness. You feel stuck in a downward spiral, feeling depressed, and then feeling depressed about feeling depressed. On bad days, you might feel really hopeless and even want to die.

If this sounds like you, and it's been going on for 2 weeks or more, you are probably suffering from depression. The good news is that depression—especially when it follows a loss—is temporary and very treatable. Here are the indicators that your blues have evolved into a depressive episode:

1. Most of the time, on most days, you feel depressed.

2. You've lost interest in most activities, and things you enjoyed before are no longer pleasurable. Again, this is happening most of the time on most days.

3. You've noticed a major appetite surge or loss, or your body weight has changed more than 5 percent in a month (without dieting).

4. You're losing sleep or sleeping too much.

5. You're either agitated or slowed down—to the extent that others can notice.

6. You feel tired and low on energy nearly every day.

7. On most days, you are plagued by guilt and/or feelings of worthlessness.

8. You're having a hard time thinking and concentrating, and/or can't seem to make decisions.

9. You find yourself thinking about death and either imagining or considering suicide.

Now, we all feel some of these things on some days, but if you've been experiencing five or more of these debilitating symptoms (including item one or two) nearly every day in a 2-week period, then you most likely have a mental health condition called Major Depression.

Do this now: get the name of a psychologist, professional counselor, or psychiatrist (ask people you trust, or just check the Yellow Pages), and then call and set up an appointment. If you can't get in soon, call someone else. You may want to set up more than one appointment so you can find the best match.

If you are thinking of hurting yourself, call 911 or go directly to the closest emergency room. Major depression is no different than any other serious illness. It's not just "in your head." It's draining your body and your spirit. Take care of it.

 Breakup Bytes

> Studies consistently show that psychotherapy and medication are both effective in treating depression, and many people use a combination of both. A psychologist or counselor will help you talk things through and develop new coping skills. A psychiatrist will evaluate your symptoms and help you find relief through medication (some psychiatrists provide counseling as well). Why not arm yourself with both? Your therapist can get you an appointment with a psychiatrist or help you obtain a prescription through your regular doctor. When life has you down, it's great to have a team on your side.

Depression is not an either/or thing: There are milder versions that also deserve attention. Bottom line is, if you're having trouble coping on your own, don't suffer. Get help!

Seeing Red: Dealing With Anger

A healthy dose of anger can be a good sign, indicating that you care about yourself and aren't willing to put up with mistreatment. But when you're spending your days developing plots for the ex's destruction, it's you who's in trouble.

Anger can feel as heavy as depression. Here you're trying to live your life and *he* pops into your head; then you start getting steamed. You tell yourself that he's not worth it, but does that help? NO. Instead, you obsess over the ways he mistreated you, hate the fact that he seems happy, review old scenes in your head, and, of course, list the 101 clever retorts you could have flung but didn't.

Who's this anger hurting? Knowing the answer to that only makes you angrier, and you feel stuck with a feeling you can't seem to shake. Here are some strategies you can use to shake it:

- **Put it on paper.** Get it out and onto the pages of your journal. Don't hold anything back. Writing it down will often help you clarify what it is that's getting to you.

- **Write the unsendable.** Draft a letter you'll *never send* that tells him everything you are feeling and imagining right now. Be as out there as you can. Exaggerate if you like.

- **Get to the bottom of it.** List everything you can think of that's making you mad. Then go back over your list and circle the hottest item. Is this something you've gotten mad about before? What can you learn from this?

- **Get a witness.** Sometimes we just need someone to hear our story. Make sure it's someone who's up for it. If you've burned out your friends, see a therapist.

- **Make it funny.** Exaggerated anger can be quite entertaining. Share the over-the-top version of your anger with your friends or complain to them "loudly" via e-mail. Seeing the ridiculous lengths you've gone to helps expose the humor of the situation and lightens things up.

- **Get over it.** If the anger dance is familiar for you, hire a therapist to help you get past it and discover some new emotions.

Filling the Void with Bad News

When you were together, there was all this "stuff" filling your life: things you did together, conversations, thoughts about him, even conflict and fights. When that's all gone, there's bound to be a void. Suddenly, you don't know what to do with yourself, and it can be scary. In our culture of cell phones, iPods, and multitasking, we are poorly equipped to deal with empty space. The natural temptation is to fill that space with something quick and easy.

So, rather than going into the void with the help of a therapist, we find helpers in the form of liquor, junk food, shopping, or sex. While all of these therapies can provide a quick fix, as a longer-term solution they only add to the pain.

Eat, Drink, and Be Not-So-Merry

The impulse to fill the void can feel like hunger. You may have just eaten, but you want more. What you feel is not that scratchy tummy-hunger that indicates it's time to eat, but an emotional emptiness. And you're probably telling yourself that you "can't stand" that feeling. So you eat. It feels good to fill the space, so you eat a lot. At some point, you notice that you are uncomfortably full. Then you feel guilty and regretful and start beating yourself up. You may swear to starve yourself or make any number of mean promises to yourself.

 Lonely Street

> The opposite of "filling up," self-deprivation, is also connected to depression. Withdrawal and isolation keep you stuck in your depressed mood, poor eating deprives you of energy, and lack of stimulation feeds boredom. You need nutrition from outside of yourself: the kind you get from the food groups, as well as the kind you get from friends, interests, physical activity, and accomplishments.

The desire to drink may go beyond the need to fill up, and include the wish to forget or be someone else. So we drink—a lot—and maybe we do forget for awhile. We act stupid, have some laughs, or just drink ourselves to sleep. What a clever solution!

Oops—we forgot something. Alcohol is a depressant! Once the fun wears off, we feel like crap, both emotionally and physically. And we do the guilty, beating-ourselves-up bit. Which, of course, makes us want to drink to escape *these* feelings, and we start digging ourselves into a big rut.

Retail Therapy

For women, filling our closets can be as tempting as filling our tummies or killing our brain cells. "Oh," we think, "those strappy sandals would help me feel sexy and make everything all better!" No matter that we've maxed the credit card with other items that promised to make it all better. When retail therapy goes beyond a fun outing (shopping is supposed to be fun!) and becomes a drug, it's time to notice what's happening.

As with other addictive behaviors, you are getting immediate emotional gain followed by a growing level of long-term pain. Soon comes the familiar guilt, the remorse, the self-flagellation. And, of course, the putting off of feelings that you could be facing and getting over. As you fill your closets and empty your bank account, you start to hem yourself in with "stuff." What once felt liberating becomes a prison of clutter and debt.

Sex "Therapy"

Let's be clear: real sex therapy helps couples develop a more rewarding sexual relationship. Having sex to cover the pain of a breakup is *not* therapy—it's another form of bad news.

Yet, the reasons we use sex are understandable: we crave comfort, affirmation of our attractiveness—or perhaps we just crave sex! Unfortunately, sex alone rarely fills the void. In fact, we can feel more alone than ever the morning after. Repeat guilt, feeling crappy, needing another fix.

From Filling Up to Showing Up

There is probably an endless list of the behaviors we can use to fill up the space left by a breakup. We can pour ourselves into our work, become addicted to TV, or get hooked on gambling. Any behavior that digs us into a cycle of self-abuse is bad news. So, how do we get out of the rut?

Let's start with that impulse to fill the void. When you feel that impulse, there is probably a message in your head that you "can't stand" the emptiness. Watch for the "can't stand" message, because it's a lie. Unless you have fallen dead or experienced spontaneous combustion, you *are* standing it. Replace "can't stand" with "don't like," which is more accurate, and you'll probably calm down. We *can* stand things we don't like, and as we stand them, we feel stronger.

Sometimes the task is to just stand it. Instead of going out drinking (again), let yourself spend a Friday night at home. When you want to pig out, shop 'till you drop, or drink away the emptiness, feel the desire without giving in to it.

Think of this as strength training. When we don't give in to an impulse, our anxiety increases, just like our heart rate increases when we work out. But the good news is that once the anxiety peaks, it sort of gives up and goes away. And the more you allow the anxiety to peak and diminish, the less anxiety you feel—and the more you realize that you are okay. And once you experience being okay without the "fillers," you'll have the power to wait for the good stuff—and the good men!

As you're resisting that binge or sexual tryst, you don't have to just sit in a heap and mope. Try investigating the emptiness. Why fill it before you even know what you need? If you look into the emptiness, you may find that what you're craving is not a bag of cookies but a friend, or rest, or a better life.

A great exercise is to grab a paper and pen instead of the filler and to write down what you're craving. Write exactly what you'd have if your fairy godmother was on hand. Maybe you want a soul mate with dark eyes and a bit of stubble on his chin: write it down and elaborate. Or maybe what you want is a different feeling in your body: write it down and elaborate. Maybe what you want is wild and impractical: write it down and elaborate.

If writing's not your thing, call an objective friend and tell her you need to talk rather than act on the impulse. Ask her to help you identify what you're really looking for. As you open up the emptiness, you'll start to realize that it's not emptiness at all, but possibility.

Here's another tip for dealing with empty space: imagine that in exactly 1 week, you are guaranteed to be in a head-over-heels, full-time relationship. This perspective might help you see the emptiness as a gift, as time to regroup, get organized, or just enjoy the quiet. The reality is, your world *can* change in a day. See if you can appreciate the opportunity you have right now.

If you suspect you have a true addiction—for example, you cannot stop drinking once you start—there are all kinds of supports out there to help: Alcoholics Anonymous, Overeaters Anonymous, Gamblers Anonymous, Debtor's Anonymous, Sex Addicts Anonymous. There are treatment programs for eating disorders and substance abuse, as well as many therapists who specialize in the treatment of addictions.

It can be hard to admit you have a problem, but the exciting prospect of treating an addiction is that it opens up your world again. Recovering alcoholics are often overwhelmed by feelings of aliveness and vitality, and recognize that they stopped developing emotionally when they started drinking. It is never too late to say "No" to bad news and "Yes" to life.

Falling Apart Repair

Whether the source is sadness, anger, or emptiness, there are times when the feeling overwhelms us and we become drenched in tears. Here are some tips for getting through it:

- **Know that this is temporary.** When we're in it, we worry we'll never get out, but we do. Feelings come on like a wave, build to a peak and then diminish. You can't see beyond it now, but there is a beyond.

- **Act smart.** This is *not* the time to call the ex or drink yourself to oblivion. If you feel a need to do something, make it positive: ask a friend or family member to come over, or check out Appendix A for lots of other options.

- **Remember that cracking isn't all bad.** Think of times in the past when a low point helped you turn things around. A crack in our defenses leaves an opening for others to come in, and also challenges us to expand.

Friends Who Are Fans

When you're falling apart, be sure to talk to a fan rather than a judge. Some friends call us on our stuff and challenge us with suggestions. Don't call them right now. Save your judging friends—and I really don't mean that in a bad way—for later when you are stable and ready for input.

For now, call the friend who is able to just be with you: the one who just listens, provides unconditional support, believes in you no matter what, and mirrors your reality rather than imposing her own. Don't rule out a family member who fits this description. The important thing is to call on someone who is not going to heap more on you right now.

You've probably experienced the "help" of a friend who offers a list of suggestions or, worse, tries to help you look on the "bright side." You end up feeling more burdened—because she's given you more to do—and guilty—because you don't *feel* happy. Be choosey when you're in distress. Bring in someone who reminds you of how terrific you are—just the way you are.

Self-Esteem Food

Rather than carelessly filling yourself just to get full, feed your love for you. Do something that makes you proud, whether it's passing on the nachos, balancing the checkbook, or going to the gym. Sometimes it's the little things that make a big difference, like getting up and taking a shower rather than staying in bed.

Sometimes you just need to be reminded of what you love about you. Get in observation mode and watch your life. You know how you notice things differently right after an inspiring movie? You can capitalize on this by seeing a movie alone and lingering in the post-movie glow. Walk to a coffee shop and drink in the world around you. Reflect on your life and those who love you. Watch your thoughts by writing them down.

Breakup Repair

When we feel bad, we often get the reward of "getting out of things." We call in sick or cancel out on social engagements. This may feel good at first, but it ultimately feeds depression. Responsibilities keep us invested in life and help us know we are making a contribution. When we avoid responsibilities, we deprive ourselves of the satisfaction of accomplishment and the good feelings that come with being connected to something larger than ourselves.

Connecting with a larger source of love, whether nature or a spiritual presence, can help recover a sense of our value and purpose. And pets are great for providing unconditional love.

Finding out what feeds love—within and without—is a lifetime process. You can even keep a "love log," jotting down the choices you make and then what you feel. Become an expert on loving yourself!

An Objective Friend: A Therapist

There is no better food than attention, and a good therapist has a lot of it to give. As with your best friend, you can talk about your deepest, darkest secrets. What's different, though, is that you get all the airtime. A therapist's office is one place where it really is all about you. Also, because the therapist has no prior relationship with you, he or she is not bored with your story, is not entangled in your story, will not be shocked or offended by your story, and has a perspective that people close to you cannot give you.

Sharing difficulties with your therapist can protect friendships from burnout and from the strain that comes when friends tell you something you don't want to hear. Finally, a therapist is trained to deal with your low points and can help you when you can't see a way out.

Although different from a friendship, the client-therapist bond can be very strong and is a big part of what makes the therapy work. So take the time to find someone you can connect with. If possible, get personal recommendations; then talk with two or three different therapists before you decide.

Medicating the Right Way

We don't set out to become addicted to something. We grab bad solutions as an attempt to find relief. For example, alcohol, with its mellowing qualities, might be the only "medicine" for anxiety that we have on hand. It's not the best solution, but the desire to relieve suffering is healthy. If you suffer from recurring anxiety or depression, real medicine is available. Schedule an appointment with a psychiatrist and find out about the good stuff! Here's how to get the most out of your visit:

- Prepare a list of any medications you currently use, including any illegal ones. Your doctor is there to help you, not judge you, and leaving something out can be dangerous.

- Track your moods and symptoms. Use the time between now and your appointment to log your moods (for example, morning, afternoon, and evening each day), sleep schedule, eating patterns, and the ways you are self-medicating. The more information you provide, the better your doctor will be able to help you.

- Write a list of questions, and be sure you get them all answered. You'll want to know about various medication options, how long it takes to feel the effects, and any potential side effects.

- Be patient. Medications for depression and anxiety can take up to several weeks to provide relief; and you may need to go through more than one trial before you and your doctor arrive at the right medication and dosage. There are so many medications available these days: hang in there until you find what works. You are worth it!

Get Over It!

Even feeling bad can be an addiction. We can get used to complaining, getting attention for our misery, and hanging out with negative people. As the old Pink Floyd song suggests, we can become "comfortably numb." If you're getting bored with your sad story, great! Boredom is a reliable clue that you are ready to move on.

A trick from Alcoholics Anonymous is to act *as if* you are where you want to be. So if you want to be in love, act as if you're in love—and hopefully you *are* in love with yourself! Feel the excitement, the lightness in your step, the sense of possibility. If it feels weird or made up, don't sweat it: just keep acting!

As you practice being the person who has what you want, start *doing* what that person would do. If you would be out of your house more, get out! If you would be tending more to your appearance, do it. If you would keep your place picked up for your lover, do that, too.

The cool thing is, now you have set the stage for having what you want—in this case, love. Rather than waiting for Mr. Awesome to come to your place and pull you out of your bed and out of the blues, you're out brushing shoulders with men, looking and feeling great!

Hmmm, seems you've upped the odds quite a bit. Meanwhile, you already have the feelings and lifestyle you crave! So get over it, or rather, act *as if* you're over it!

The Least You Need to Know

- Depression, like most illness, is temporary and treatable.

- Holding on to anger only hurts you.

- Understand your emptiness rather than trying to fill it up.

- A "solution" that destroys is an addiction.

- Choose activities that increase self-love and put you where you want to be.

Rejection 101

In This Chapter

- The secret to the best prospects
- Practicing getting rejected
- The importance of rejecting
- Creating a prototype of your match
- Internet dating as sorting practice

So why is a course in rejection coming at this point in the book? The reason is simple: the better you can handle rejecting and being rejected, the better the prospects ahead. Confused?

This chapter will help you overcome the fear of rejection and free you to ask for what you want from relationships.

Rejection as a Side Effect of Living

Think of the people who have made it big. If you look into their histories, you will probably find a higher-than-average number of rejections. Famous actors, authors, athletes, and entrepreneurs have similar stories of the repeated rejections they endured. While it wasn't easy, somewhere along the way, these individuals got tough: they accepted rejection as a necessary part of getting to the Big Time.

Though we don't all aspire to be famous, we can learn something from people who do. These go-getters tend to share the following qualities:

- They enjoy taking risks and not knowing what will happen.

- They find the *process* entertaining, and don't just wait for outcomes.

- They don't take rejection too personally. From experience, they learn success is more a matching game (what you want and what they want) than a "who's worthy" contest.

- They are optimistic and see abundance where others see scarcity.

- They don't settle.

Desensitizing Yourself

Let's look at a few post-breakup scenarios:

Scenario 1: *Jane dates a Dick who acts like he's God's gift to women. Because Jane has already been rejected, she does everything she can to avoid another dump job. Two rejections in a row would be devastating!*

Scenario 2: *Jane dates the same Dick. He IS hot, and she likes him but hates his attitude. She decides to tell him that although she really likes him, his aloofness leaves her feeling dismissed. She knows he could be offended and break it off. If he does, that confirms that he's not worth her effort, and she'll be better off.*

Scenario 3: *Jane dates the same Dick. While she likes him, she feels she could get Dick minus the bad attitude. She calls it off.*

Notice that in Scenario 1, Jane's behavior is controlled by her fear of rejection. In Scenario 2, Jane accepts the risk of rejection by asking for more. In Scenario 3, Jane welcomes breakup #2 and goes for the gold!

Sensitivity to rejection is one of the biggest barriers to finding great relationships. Avoiding rejection requires us to avoid being truthful, avoid our desires, and ultimately avoid relationships.

So how do we desensitize? Simple: practice getting rejected. Yes, I'm serious. Look for opportunities to go out on a limb and risk rejection. You don't need to *try* to be rejected, but put yourself in situations where the odds are against you. Introduce yourself to the guy everyone wants to date. Audition for a lead role in a big local production. Try to "convert" the wish-he-wasn't-gay hottie. Put $20 on the number 20.

You only get points when you come up with nothing, and the higher the number of rejections, the better. Enjoy being a little careless and trusting that there is enough: enough time, enough men, enough opportunity. Keep track of your rejections, and reward yourself when you reach 5, 10, or 20. Seem like a lot? One therapist desensitized himself by asking out 100 complete strangers in Central Park. While I don't recommend this, it worked for him. And he even got some dates!

Breakup Bytes

The movie, *How to Lose a Guy in 10 Days,* provides a great demonstration of how to boldly pursue rejection. The main character, Andie, indulges herself freely in all the turn-off behaviors she advises her friends to avoid: from calling him incessantly to bringing cucumber sandwiches to his guys-only poker game. The playful movie takes the pursuit of rejection to an extreme, yet shows there may be more room for mistakes than we realize. On the other hand, her psycho-stalker gig may have a pretty high rate of success (in achieving rejection, that is). Andie not only desensitizes herself to rejection, but she also makes it her specialty. Watching the movie provides vicarious desensitization, and reminds us that love often happens when we're focused on something else. Ready to try losing a guy?

It's a challenging shift to see rejection as a prize, so keep your sense of humor. Use your best rejection stories to entertain your friends. Have you noticed how some people can turn around an extremely embarrassing moment and render it cool as they tell about it? It takes confidence to acknowledge rejection. When you do, people see that your self-esteem is not based on whether a particular person approves of you.

Okay, so all of this is easier said than done. You'll probably still feel the "ouch" when you get the brush-off, which is why it's crucial to keep your support system strong. Gather a cheering section of friends to applaud your efforts; maybe some of them will pursue rejections with you!

Increasing Your Odds

When you add low-odds situations to your safer attempts to get connected, it's like diversifying in business. You cover more bases and increase your chances of hitting it big! When you think about it, finding matches is always an odds game. It's hard to explain what magic combination of elements makes someone just right for you. But it's easy to understand that the more people you meet and the more you extend your reach, the more likely you are to find that magic.

The way you do this is to get out more, collect your target number of rejections, but also play some safe bets. This sets up a win-win situation: rejections desensitize you, easy bets stroke your ego, and awesome hits may take you by surprise! Maybe you'll discover that the presumed gay hottie is actually very straight, or that the guy all the women want only wants *you*.

When you take a long-term perspective (easier said than done), rejection is your friend. Think back, or ask around: most of us can list rejections we are grateful for. There's a great song by Sister Hazel honoring such a rejection. It's a thank-you note to the ex for teaching the songwriter "what I *don't* need." How many of us would have settled for an alcoholic, or a cheater, or a poverty-stricken moocher, if he hadn't moved on?

If either one of you decides to end it, that relationship was not enough. Would you really be happy having a hunk around who didn't find you very attractive? Or is it enough to be adored if you don't respect your partner? The process of acceptance and rejection, while painful, is essential to finding mutual fulfillment. You—and the people you date—are developing a definition of what works, and this can only happen as you go. In this respect, the more dating, sorting, and rejecting you go through, the better!

In addition to helping you define what you want (and don't want), the dating-and-rejection process also helps you *find* it. We have this strange idea that we should be able to bypass experience and get right to the perfect match. That's like expecting to find the right college or apartment by only visiting one, and then criticizing yourself if it doesn't work out! Think of all the people in the world; then think of how many you've dated. Quite a gap, huh? Perhaps there's room for a little more exploration.

Learning to Reject

If avoidance of rejection undermines your chances of finding good matches, difficulty doing the rejecting can be even more of an obstacle. You may have had the good fortune of being *rejected* by a loser, but, if you can't reject a loser who's hanging on, you're stuck.

Rejecting someone who's bad for you is hard enough, but rejecting a great person who's not great for *you* is even harder. It takes faith to reject: faith that there's more out there, and faith that you can do better. It's time to believe!

Abundance Thinking

How you see the world has a big effect on how you view your options. If you see scarcity, you hold on to what you have or grab what you can get, even if it's not great. If you see abundance, you are more picky and willing to give up "good" in order to find "great!"

So how do you see abundance? Like anything, abundance thinking requires practice. Start by catching your thoughts. Does the inside of your head sound something like this?

- I'll never find what I'm looking for.
- All the guys in this town/state/world are losers.
- Why don't I face reality? (Assumption: reality = suffering.)

- Love only happens in fairy tales.

- I have rotten luck; nothing ever works out for me.

- I expect too much; I'm too picky!

Lonely Street

As you master the art of rejecting, you may hear the words "you're too picky" from people around you—or from inside your own head. Unless you are crazy about the one you're with, *and* he is crazy about you, *and* he treats you very well, you are not being too picky. You may find that the people who accuse you of being picky are ones who have settled for less in their own lives. (Of course, you don't have to tell them that.)

It's a big step to just catch these thoughts and to question them rather than accept them as truth. The next step is to replace these "scarcity thoughts" with "abundance thoughts." Try these:

- There is enough for everyone.

- The world is conspiring in my favor.

- "Nothing is too wonderful to be true." —Michael Faraday

- Loving matches are made every day.

- If I desire more, I will receive more.

Create some abundant thoughts of your own, and add them to the mix. Read through the list every morning, or pick your favorite and put it on a sticky note on your mirror, refrigerator, or car dash.

Maybe you don't believe these words right now. That's okay. As you practice viewing life and love from the perspective of abundance, you will begin to see things differently. You will give credibility to what you want, rather than viewing your desires as silly or frivolous.

Another great way to practice believing is to keep an "Abundance Journal." At the end of every day, write down what went well, what you love about your life, what you have that others desire. Your items can be as simple as "laughing with Joanne at lunch" or as global as "my great sense of humor." If you have a tough day, you may be just grateful to get through it. Write that down, and see if you can note the qualities or people that helped you get through.

Airplane pilots learn that if they focus on what they *don't* want to hit, they actually increase the likelihood of hitting it. They learn instead to concentrate on where they want to go. Your focus becomes your reality, so aim for abundance!

Holding Out for Great!

What are you looking for? Maybe you haven't even thought about it. After a breakup, we are often most in touch with what we *don't* want. While this is important information, it's only the beginning.

Remember, you are free! There's a world of possibilities available to you (even if you don't see them now). Do you want to close down your options by grabbing for something safe, or even "good"?

What about great? By "great," I mean a great match: the kind that compels you to spend as much time as possible with each other; the kind that feels amazingly comfortable and exciting at the same time; the kind that has you both feeling blessed by luck.

Great is *not* what everyone *else* defines as great (though it could be), and it's not usually someone who defines himself as great (though this could be, too). *Great* is that chemical, emotional, spiritual—or use your own word—reaction that happens between you and someone who matches your unique desires (and visa versa). If you don't get this, you could be wasting your time pursuing people who look good to others, but don't really excite *you*. These people may get a lot of up-front action, but they often have a hard time matching up with anyone. This is because they're all form and little substance. And it is substance that will make your world turn upside down.

To help you identify your match, create your own prototype. Here's where your dating experience will help.

1. Make a list of everyone you've dated.

2. Next to each name, write down the quality or qualities you want to take from that person for your prototype: "the way he kissed me," or "his spontaneity."

3. If a name reminds you of a quality you *don't* want, see if its opposite belongs in your prototype. For example, if you hate cheapness, then generosity may be what you're looking for.

4. Now list qualities you have not yet experienced, but have impressed you. Perhaps it's the way your friend's boyfriend looks at her, or the way a movie character teases his lover.

5. Don't forget to list physical qualities that attract you. Again, try to use real people as guides, because they can reveal subtleties we otherwise overlook. Maybe Joaquin Phoenix's dark, brooding quality attracts you because it represents intensity, or a surfer blond look reminds you of fun and spontaneity.

6. Expand your list as you collect new information. Each date is a potential source of data, as are the observations you make every day. Try not to judge or water down what you like, because you might just edit out the things that make him yours!

A friend of mine, with the help of her exes, created a very detailed description of the love of her life. She put it away in a drawer. Recently, she started dating a man who seemed like an answer to her every wish. To check it out, she pulled out the list. Except for a couple of minor items, he matches on every item! Here are a few of the characteristics of her prototype (and now, real-life love!):

- **Loyal:** *His desire to be a loyal friend always outweighs his need to save face, impress others, or win popularity. He doesn't need to puff up his ego with the attention of other women. He would never cheat. Is proud to have me in his life and never denies that he's in an exclusive relationship with me. Wants to be with me as much as I want to be with him, and misses me when we're apart.*

- **Secure:** *Finds it easy to say he's sorry, or at least that he understands that I could feel the way I do. Is not threatened by my honesty, respects my thinking process, and is not defensive or sarcastic when I express myself. Knows how to redirect and minimize conflict, and not intensify an already-hurtful situation. Gives me my space and does not try to control me.*

- **Considerate:** *He calls when he says he will, returns my calls, communicates and makes plans that include my input and desires, and respects my property and belongings.*

- **Independent:** *Has friends of his own, interests outside of me, carries a sense of complexity and intrigue, not easily mastered.*

- **Financially secure:** *His love for himself has resulted in sound financial decisions, his talent has produced the fruit of success, he loves to pay the tab when we go out, and take care of me in a somewhat old-fashioned sense.*

Helen Fielding's book-made-movie, *Bridget Jones' Diary*, offers an entertaining example of the difference between superficial "great" and "great match."

If you haven't seen it, skip the next three paragraphs and rent it tonight!

The movie's heroine (Bridget) has to suffer betrayal by the great-looking, smooth swinger (played by Hugh Grant), in order to notice the handsome, but not always smooth, man who steals her heart (played by Colin Firth). The affection between Firth's character, Mark Darcy, and Bridget is based on the whole interesting package rather than surface charm. As they each admit their interest, acceptance meets humor:

Mark Darcy: I don't think you're an idiot at all. I mean, there are elements of the ridiculous about you. Your mother's pretty interesting. And you really are an appallingly bad public speaker. And, um, you tend to let whatever's in your head come out of your mouth without much consideration of the consequences ... but the thing is, um, what I'm trying to say, very inarticulately, is that, um, in fact, perhaps despite appearances, I like you, very much. Just as you are.

Bridget: You once said you liked me just as I am and I just wanted to say likewise. I mean there are stupid things your mum buys you—tonight's another ... classic. You're haughty, and you always say the wrong thing in every situation and I seriously believe that you should rethink the length of your sideburns. But, you're a nice man and I like you. If you wanted to pop by some time that might be nice .... More than nice.

Breakup Repair

> Finding someone *else* who accepts you fully may be difficult if you don't accept yourself fully. Think of the confession of love in a romantic comedy: that list of the endearing little quirks he loves about her (or vice versa). Now write a confession of love to yourself. Start with "I love the way you _____," and see what you come up with. Regarding these qualities as adorable rather than weird or embarrassing can transform the way you carry yourself.

Great matches happen when you have the courage to say no to "Good," *and* to someone else's version of "Great." Move on, girl, and meet your match.

Rejections in Cyberspace

Without knowing it, the online dating industry has created a great rejection-desensitization tool. In the safety of your own home, you can scan all kinds of dating options and pick which ones to follow up on. And, if you have a profile, you get scanned, too. Then you follow up with matches, but you are still just "checking them out" and they you. Participants develop ways of rejecting that they can live with, and don't usually get too bent out of shape when they get the letdown message.

Online dating puts us all in the same boat. No longer does boy only ask out girl, but both check each other out. No longer does the interested party need to guess about whether to approach someone: the impartial computer tells you if there's a green light.

So even if you prefer traditional ways of meeting people, signing up with an Internet dating service (many are free!) can help you:

1. Develop hope just by seeing the massive number of people who are looking.
2. Identify what you like and don't like.
3. Practice rejecting.
4. Practice getting rejected.

So, how do you go about letting someone down after a few emails or phone calls, or even the first meeting? The e-mail stage is the simplest, though you may find yourself devising multiple drafts before pressing "Send."

As we discussed in Chapter 2, keep your message short and to the point. For example, here's a message that covers the majority of situations: "I enjoyed getting to know you, but I'm not feeling that connection I'm looking for." The easiest and most digestible feedback emphasizes the *lack of fit* rather than a defect in the other person.

If you're at the "talking by phone" stage of Internet dating, break up by phone. As a general rule, communicate the breakup at the level you have been communicating your interest. However, if you've just met once to check each other out, it would be awkward to schedule a second meeting just to dump him. Instead, give him a call or send an e-mail if that has been your primary way of communicating.

Another common way to end an online relationship is to stop e-mailing or calling. This is the wimpy way out. Just end it! You'll spare yourself the carpel tunnel you might develop from repeatedly pressing the "Delete" button and, most important, you'll be treating the other person with the respect you would want for yourself.

We've probably talked enough about how to handle being on the receiving end of the send-off. There's probably no better teacher than experience; with online dating, you can get as much as you want!

The Least You Need to Know

- If you want the best options, expect some rejections.
- Deliberately getting rejected helps you become less sensitive.
- As with other investments, diversification pays.
- An attitude of abundance leaves room for rejecting good guys.
- Look for a great match rather than a "great" person.
- Try the Internet for selection and rejection experience.

Chapter 9

Stepping Back

In This Chapter

- Asking "Why?" again
- Looking at your role
- Overcoming denial
- Getting comfy with desire
- Loving you

Remember all the work we did to quiet the repeating "Why?" in your head? Well, now's the time to revive the question. Once the intensity has quieted down and you have stopped fighting the reality of your breakup, you're in a better position to evaluate what happened. In contrast to your initial Whys—back when you didn't really want to know—your questions can now find answers. Just as we are better able to see the landscape after reaching the top of the hill, we get the best perspective on old relationships after getting some distance from them.

Another advantage of asking now is that you are less preoccupied with your ex's actions. Asking "Why?" about what he does is futile; asking "Why?" about what you do is crucial.

Exploring the tough questions now, when things have cooled off, will prepare you to make better choices when things heat up in a new relationship. When our emotions run high, we're at risk of losing perspective. That could happen sooner than you think, so let's seize the day and find some answers!

Relationship Review

If I ask you what mistakes your good friend or sibling makes when it comes to relationships, you probably won't miss a beat in providing a thorough analysis. But you may feel stumped when the question is directed to you. Or else you may know the answer, but still feel stuck in the behavior patterns that cause problems.

Let's look at two common relationship-busters: denying problems and repeating old roles.

Was I Really *Happy*?

Was it really all that great? Did his occasional good moods compensate for all the times he was short with you, critical, and generally negative? Did his great smile make up for his poor taste and crude behavior?

Maybe the pluses did outweigh the minuses—but then he cheated on you. He Cheated On You! So why are you keeping him in the "wanted" column? He Cheated On You! Do you really want a cheater?

It can be incredibly hard to see what is right there in front of us, not because it isn't obvious, but because we don't want to see. We insist on staying in the game, but the biggest game we're playing is with ourselves, and the name of the game is denial.

Denial is a way of extending a fantasy when reality gets in the way. When you like someone, you develop a story about the person and your relationship. And it's not just any story: it's a really good one. But you don't see it as a story; you feel it in your heart and soul, and you want it more than anything. Let's look at an example:

Let's say you meet a person who seems to be a really good listener. His way of attending to your words moves you, and you build a story out of this experience. You tell yourself about how he will make you feel safe enough to share your deepest pain, and how that sharing will heal you.

So, on your next date, you talk about your tough childhood, and he seems interested enough. He even shares a few things about his past. You decide to tell him some things you haven't even told your best friend. He nods his head and seems to be listening, though you get a little sense that he might be bored. Well, that's your fault—you're not digging deep enough. So you share more and now he's clearly restless and distracted. You tell yourself he's just emotionally exhausted.

If you're really committed to the Tale of the Good Listener, he could get up and leave in the middle of the conversation, and you'd conclude that he's overcome with emotion, or that you still aren't telling it right—anything that fits with your internal script. Meanwhile, he is showing you the truth: he is not the healer you made him out to be.

The example may seem laughable, but this kind of self-deception happens all the time. We don't set out to lie to ourselves. We build the story out of very powerful impressions, and the tale takes on a life of its own. Without even recognizing what's happening, we become very committed to the story. That's where denial comes in.

Think back on the story you told yourself about your relationship with your ex. What qualities did your ex reveal that were inconsistent with your story? Were you willfully blind to those qualities? Did you blame yourself for them? What did you edit out and what did you enhance? Were you in love with him or with the story?

To take it a step further, use two columns to contrast the story with the reality. In the left column, write down the qualities he was supposed to have according to the story. In the right column, write down the qualities revealed by his behavior. Teasing apart what was real and what wasn't is good practice for new relationships.

The good news is that some stories do match up with reality, and many real stories are better than what we can imagine. The trick is to allow *reality* to shape the drama, rather than the other way around. The surprises and inconsistencies might let us down or thrill us. Either way, you're better off seeing them clearly.

My Part in the Tango

When you're in a relationship, you and your partner begin a dance. You each bring to it what you know, and your steps become coordinated. The dance flows as long as both of you keep in step. But what if you're into salsa and the dance is a waltz? You may get bored with that 1-2-3 rhythm, and wish he would start to shake it up. But you keep waltzing. Meanwhile, he wants to tango, but the waltz is going so well, he's afraid to mess it up. You're both unhappy, but at least the waltz is comfortable and easy. That is, until one of you decides to find a new partner.

So why did you choose the waltz to begin with? Maybe you watched your parents waltz all the time when you were little and the rhythm got inside you. Maybe you've already mastered the waltz and you're still insecure with salsa. Or maybe you didn't want to lead, so you just followed his.

It does take two to tango, and to waltz. If you had a mother-son type of dance, his step may have been the helpless act, but your step of providing help was also essential. If, instead of being helpful, you had shrugged your shoulders and said, "Heck if I know," you would have thrown him off. Sure, he might have tried harder to keep you in step, but the next move would still have been yours.

What steps did you bring into the relationship that helped form the dance? Did your need to be needed harmonize with his helplessness? Did your investment in being the smart one shine next to his limited conversation skills? Did your habit of being the reformer draw you to his bad-boy behavior?

Without knowing it, we often attract deficiencies to help us feel superior, successful, or generous. We can also attract superheroes who rescue us but also undermine our competence. Either way, the steps keep us in the same place rather than helping us grow.

See if you can come up with a name for the dance between you and your ex, like the Absent Partner Dance (one of you checks out a lot while the other waits on the sidelines) or the Bad Boy Shuffle (he knocks into people and you apologize). Note the steps you needed to perform in order to make the dance flow. Then decide if you want to do this dance in the next relationship. If not, are you willing to learn some new steps or to have a more flexible routine? After all, dancing at its best is about movement, self-expression, and artistically finding a way to be both an individual and part of a couple. And, more than anything, it's about having fun!

Learning from Mistakes

We might cringe a little—or a lot!—as we look back. It's not fun to focus on our mistakes. Yet, nothing teaches as well as a big, fat screw-up. When the past makes us cringe, we're more motivated to do things differently next time. By contrast, when we avoid the discomfort of looking back, we can happily continue to repeat our mistakes. So, by cringing now, you may avoid being mortified later.

Actually, it's a good idea to make friends with our mistakes. It's hard to know what kind of dance we prefer until we try out a variety of steps and partners. With every relationship, we get a better idea of what we like and what we don't.

The point is not to stop making mistakes, but to make *new* mistakes rather than repeat old ones—and therefore, learn new lessons. When you're in a relationship, it's important to stay conscious and re-evaluate the dance at regular intervals. Good partnerships are flexible: there's room for stepping on toes, shifting, and learning new steps. After all, if the steps can't be changed, you're in a prison—not a relationship.

Be prepared. Your new dance may not be as elegant or smooth. In her song, *Foreign Soul*, singer-songwriter Rebecca describes the challenge of dancing with desire:

> *Used to move my way through like a dancer,*
> *staying in step, staying in line.*
> *Now I'm daring and stumbling and falling*
> *out of synch, out of time.*

Trying new steps may feel awkward and foreign, and you won't always know what comes next. But just as you learned the old role, you can get good at new ones. Better yet, you can get good at change, learning from mistakes and shifting in response.

Relationship skills develop over a lifetime. Instead of looking for the perfect steps, try moving to the music inside you!

The Courage to Want More

What kind of partner do you desire? How do you want him to treat you? What kinds of behaviors would thrill you? How would you like him to touch you?

If you're getting uncomfortable with these questions, you may be keeping your desires under wraps. It can be scary to expose our most powerful longings, so we store them in our fantasies, where they can't be messed with—or fulfilled.

 Lonely Street

> When you get in touch with your desire for someone new, your excitement can feel overwhelming and even uncomfortable. When this happens, the natural tendency is to (a) Shut down your desires, or (b) Impulsively try to indulge the desire. These responses actually interfere with getting what you want. Stop yourself, and practice relaxing into your desire. You need time to get it right, and faith to tolerate the wait.

Bringing desire to your choices takes courage. It might mean passing on the first and even second or third person who asks you out. It might mean approaching someone you haven't met. And it usually involves rejecting and risking being rejected. But, most of all, acting with desire means getting what you want!

It's really very simple: *ask and you get.* Ask the world for a great match and you'll recognize when you see it. Ask your partner for what you want and, if he's worth his salt, he'll appreciate your openness and want to respond. Say thank you. Simple stuff. But, oh, so hard. Here are some thoughts that mess with simple and get us scared:

1. What if there is nobody like that out there?

2. What if I meet somebody like that, but he doesn't like me?

3. What if I ask for what I want and he says no?

4. What if he thinks I'm selfish, or needy, or demanding?

5. What if he knows the truth about me and doesn't like it (or me)?

Notice that each sentence begins with "What if." These statements tend to overestimate risk and underestimate your capacity for dealing with disappointment. Let's go back over the "What ifs" and answer the questions:

1. **What if there's nobody like that out there?** *Not likely. I got my ideas from real people, so there are probably people like that out there.*

2. **What if I meet somebody like that, but he doesn't like me?** *That would be disappointing, but I'd deal with it. Then I'd look for someone who meets my desire and desires me!*

3. **What if he says no?** *That does not make my request wrong. And I have all kinds of options: if my request is not that important to me, I can let it go. If it is important, I can talk with him more, hear his side and work out a compromise, or re-evaluate the relationship.*

4. **What if he thinks I'm selfish, or needy, or demanding?** *Then the problem is with him, not me. Maybe he has a hard time allowing his own desires. It's only a problem for me if I agree with him.*

5. **What if he knows the truth about me and doesn't like it (or me)?** *One word: goodbye!*

We often see the risk in asking for more, while ignoring the risk of settling for less. Sure, we may shoot for more and end up with less; but if we settle for less, then it's *guaranteed*!

Chances are, however, that shooting for more will result in more: more adventure, more learning, and more of a relationship. The best way to deal with the doubting voice within is to overwhelm it with your desires.

Think more about more. Visualize who you want, where you are together, what you feel in your body, what you're saying and doing—make it as real as possible. Let the vision become part of you, and it will move you toward its counterpart in reality. Edit the vision as you encounter new sources of inspiration. Keep pushing the outer limits of more. Then see how big your world becomes.

Self-Affirmation: Looking Good!

So how do you build up the confidence to go for more? Simple: see the more in you. Because we hang around ourselves all of the time, we get desensitized to our own amazing qualities. That's why it's so important to step back and see ourselves through fresh eyes.

Do a little documentary on yourself (no camera necessary). Interview the people who know and love you. Ask them what they love and admire in you, from your talents and values to the way you are in relationships to your physical appearance. A really good friend might even be willing to talk about qualities she envies! A good interview will include the details, personal style, and quirks that make you uniquely loveable. Then pick a friend to interview you with the goal of finding out (a) The talents, interests, and values that have been a part of you since childhood, and (b) What you love about yourself.

Once you complete your research, notice the themes that emerge, and summarize these with key words or short phrases. For example, if people love the way you enthusiastically pour yourself into whatever you're doing, "passion" may be a key word. If people admire your brainpower, you might like "sexy brain." Pick words or phrases that you find attractive and that remind you of your best qualities.

Finally, write your key words and phrases in big letters on little notes and post them on your mirror. Remind yourself of these attractive qualities every time you get ready to go out. Wear them with pride!

The Least You Need to Know

- Analyze yourself, not your ex.
- Look at what actually *was*, not the story you told yourself.
- Identify the role you played and whether you liked it.
- Learn to be honest with yourself and change in response.
- Don't limit your expectations of what can be.
- Build confidence by looking within.

Stepping Out!

In This Chapter

- Releasing and forgiving
- Tools for keeping perspective
- Developing a sense of humor
- Where to meet people
- Commitment to your desire

If you've ever moved, you know what it's like to pack up everything you own, including the furniture and cleaning supplies, get it all into a moving van, and then unload and unpack it all at the new destination.

By contrast, going on an adventure involves leaving most of your accumulated belongings behind, while picking up some special supplies. An adventure is a special journey that requires smart preparation, but offers little information on what to expect. If you can live with these terms, you're ready to step out!

Chapter 8 helped you sort and pare down what you want to bring along; this chapter will help you get out the door and give you some tools for the trip.

Releasing the Past

So the breakup is over. You said your goodbyes, faced the differences between your ex and what you wanted him to be, and looked at your role in how things went. Now it's time to let it all go and trust what you've learned. By releasing the past, you can approach new relationships with a fresh perspective and clearer vision.

But how do you release? If the ex had died, you would at least get a funeral! There is no ceremony for a breakup, except perhaps a long night on the couch with a gallon of ice cream, or a long night at a bar with a sympathetic bartender (yeah, that one's more of a guy thing). Rituals and ceremonies, on the other hand, provide a way to acknowledge the loss, pay tribute to what was, receive support and comfort from friends and family, and obtain some closure. So how about creating a ritual or ceremony of your own? Let's look at some ways breakup survivors have released the past.

Write a Letter

This is different from the purge letter we talked about in Chapter 6. In other words, it's not mean and you can even send it. In this letter, you honor what was good about your ex and your relationship. No regrets, no resentment, no agenda—just acknowledgement and gratitude for what you had and what you learned. This way of achieving closure can be very healing, because you are making peace with the past. By letting go of the pain and honoring what remains, you are forgiving both your ex and yourself.

Host a "Relationship Funeral"

Though this may sound morbid, a relationship has died and you might want some help moving on. Invite your friends to a ceremony to honor and say goodbye to the couple you once were. Bring out photos and memorabilia if you want, play "your song," and stock plenty of tissue. You can even write a eulogy to the relationship, noting the dates of its birth and death, the highlights of its lifetime, and any sentiments you may want to express.

Bury or Burn the Past

Select an item that symbolizes your relationship, such as a gift he gave you, a photo of the two of you, or a piece of memorabilia, such as a concert ticket stub. Bury that item and formally say good-bye. You may even want to plant a seedling along with the item to represent the new life that will grow out of the remains of the relationship.

Burning the purge letter you wrote at the beginning of this process can be a wonderful way of releasing your pain and forgiving your ex.

Symbolize

Think about the purpose your relationship has served in your life, and choose an item to capture that meaning. Examples might include a candle to represent the insight you've gained, or a toy to symbolize the playfulness he brought out in you. What's nice about this approach is that you are giving yourself a gift that parallels what you acquired from the relationship. This can be a refreshing contrast to focusing on your loss.

You may have your own creative way of releasing the past. While these rituals do not substitute for the hard work of getting over a breakup, they do help provide closure so that you can move on.

 Lonely Street

> The ceremony will not help you let go if you're not ready. It is there to mark the progress you have already made in your heart. If a ritual for closure happens too early, all you do is open up old desires, unresolved questions, and bitter feelings. The ceremony is for *closure* after all, not *opening back up*. There can be pain in letting go, but it's a quiet pain, not the driven feeling that comes earlier in the process.

So let's move on! You no longer need the baggage: just grab your lipstick and some cash. The adventure of the new awaits!

Lightening Up

As you start to date again, or attempt to date again, let yourself have fun along the way. Love, drama, and comedy have a longstanding relationship. Why do you think relationship flicks are called romantic *comedies*? From Bridget Jones's smoking and drinking binges to Carrie Bradshaw's dilemmas about "Big," we sometimes only survive the heartache of love through laughter.

LOL!

A sense of humor is not only a great coping tool, it's also attractive! Humor is an important aspect of flirting (such as mutual teasing), and it can help you talk about sensitive topics (e.g., the ex or sex) without things getting too heavy. Here are some ways to build your laugh muscles:

- **Practice being funny.** Buy a good joke book and memorize your favorites. Try them out on your friends. Your date (if he has a sense of humor) will be impressed, and will probably have some jokes for you.

- **Feed yourself with humor.** Watch funny movies, get some friends together and hit a comedy club. Hang out with witty people.

- **LOL.** E-mail, IMs, blogs, and the Web are great forums for humor, because they're informal and allow for spontaneity. Trying sharing your day, complete with flub-ups and letdowns, and see if you can get a LOL back!

- **Practice honesty.** If you listen to comedians, they are often just more honest than the rest of us. They talk about their weaknesses, obsessions, and embarrassments; they comment on everyday events that strike them funny; and they love to talk about their failures in love. Try a little frankness.

- **Bring out your inner girl.** A close friend of humor is playfulness. Buy something fun for your wardrobe, wear hot pink nail polish, and flirt, flirt, flirt!

Enjoy the Drama

When we set out on the adventure of love and romance, we become part of a timeless drama. Regardless of how predictable the formula, we don't seem to tire of romantic comedies. And just about every television drama keeps our interest through sexual tension between characters.

The romantic comedy is not an invention of modern cinema. William Shakespeare wrote a number of plays in this genre, including *A Midsummer Night's Dream*, *Much Ado About Nothing*, and *As You Like It*.

The basic formula of a romantic comedy involves two people who meet and, despite obvious chemistry, either don't get along or can't hook up due to circumstances. After a series of comic interactions, they go their separate ways. Tension builds as one or both parties realize they are supposed to be together, and through overcoming a series of obstacles, they miraculously meet, confess their love for each other, and the movie ends with scenes of their joyful coupling (often a wedding). The happy ending is enhanced by its contrast with the obstacles that occur throughout the drama. Keep this in mind as you deal with the obstacles in your love life!

It is curious how we can be so entertained by romantic drama on the big and small screen, in books and in songs, yet be so impatient with romantic drama in our own lives.

What if you could sit back and watch your life as if it were a movie? You might look at escalating conflict and tension as exciting rather than distressing. You might enjoy, rather than complain about, the fact that you don't know how it will turn out. And you might have a little more faith that the story will come out okay—that the purpose of the drama will be revealed. But mostly, you'd show up for the story and really get into it!

You can practice watching your love life as if it's a movie. Here's how:

1. Schedule a time, at least once a week, to see a movie by yourself. Although you can rent a movie, the big screen is better for immersing you in the experience—and doing things alone in public is good for your self-confidence. If you can pull it off, weekday matinees are best because the theatres are usually quieter (at least on school days).

2. Allow at least 30 minutes following the show to indulge in the post-movie glow. Because you're in an observing mode, this is a great time to view your life and consider the plot unfolding for you. Head to a coffee shop or go for a walk, and ponder your drama.

3. Try writing about your life in the third person. So instead of the typical journal entry, "I talked to Matt at the gym," you might say, "Jen met Matt as she was entering the weight-training area." This shift in perspective takes you outside of the drama and enables you to observe and comment.

4. Imagine events in your life as movie scenes. If you and your date are dining at a restaurant, notice the lighting and décor. What camera angles might you select if you were directing this scene?

5. When something in your story goes wrong, view it as "plot thickener." Things have just gotten more interesting and challenging.

6. If you lose faith, remind yourself that, in this movie, everything is going to come out all right.

The best movies for life reflection are ones that draw you in through your senses, have characters you can identify with, and leave you in a thoughtful, uplifted, or inspired mood. See what's playing, or check out Appendix C for some great rental options.

Looking for Love

Now that you have the tools for your adventure, you might be wondering which way to go. Let's look at some places to explore.

Gather for a Cause

Volunteering is a great way to meet people who share similar passions. Working for a shared cause breaks down barriers and gives you something to talk about. Pet lovers can meet up by helping out at an animal shelter. Nature lovers can find each other at environmental advocacy gatherings or nature hikes. You might want to get into the excitement of a political campaign, or follow a creative yearning with a local arts organization.

Search from Home

You have the world at your disposal with the Internet, and online dating can be a great way to cover a lot of ground in a short amount of time. Look for independent reviews to help you narrow down the vast number of sites, ask friends which sites they like, and consider specialty sites if you're looking for someone of a particular religion or ethnic group.

Privately Go Public

Notice how you meet more people when you travel by yourself? The same is true of going to meeting places like coffee shops, clubs, workout facilities, and religious gatherings. If you're already talking to someone you came with, you might miss the chance to talk to someone new. However, if you are sketching or reading in a coffeehouse, you give people something to ask you about.

Breakup Repair

> Although going alone frees you to meet people, friends can be assets. Go with friends to gatherings of people they know, and ask them to introduce you around. It's also a good idea to go with friends to a bar or club. You can split up, but it's nice to have a friend there as an excuse if you get approached by someone slimy. Finally, set-ups by friends *can* work; just talk through what it will mean if it doesn't.

Hit the Books

College settings have always been prime sites for making matches. If you're not currently in school, you can still take a class at your local university. If you're on the career track, mingle with people in your profession at a conference or training workshop. Sharing ideas can be a surprising turn-on!

Join a Club

If you have an interest, there's probably a club to match. There are clubs for athletic pursuits (running, biking, tennis) and creative expression (writer's groups, gourmet cooking clubs), for sharing ideas (book clubs, discussion groups) and sharing experiences (wine tastings, exploration clubs).

Use a Service

New and creative dating services are popping up all the time. Some of them, like Speed Dating, It's Just Lunch, and Eight at Eight have become popular because they get you meeting people right away in a brief or low-pressure context, and help you avoid awkward mismatches.

Staying the Course

Finding someone you match up with can take awhile. In the meantime, you might ride a rollercoaster of feelings: boredom, frustration, hope, discouragement, emptiness, excitement, confidence, despair. If you enjoy rollercoasters, you know that excitement is a close relative of fear, and you learn to trust the course you've chosen.

Similarly, as you follow your own desires in dating, you'll do better if you allow shifting feelings to wash over you, like the wind on a fast ride. Any journey has boring spells, and times when you feel tired, and times when you're sure you won't make it. If you turned around each time you questioned your journey, and started out again when you felt hopeful, you would only walk in a circle. (Some people do!) Remember, a bad day can be just that: a bad day. It doesn't have to mean anything about your life.

The one thing you can use as a guide is your desire. Feed that desire with self-knowledge, and modify it with experience. What you want may change and cause your course to shift. Great! After all, when you are on an adventure, there is no failure, only discovery. A writer I know who had always been the giver in relationships recently shared her exhilaration with me after finding a very different kind of partner:

"He's not my type (which is good!), and I'm not his type (which is also good). He pays for stuff—he's sorry about things! And I have no reason to feel sorry for him: he's not like that. We are both so amazed! We could be like breaking each other's bad luck. He's like me—a giver. Finally, we both have what we deserve. It feels like home. This relationship is an entity: it doesn't need help. It's self-sufficient. I didn't know it could be this good!"

Staying True to You

As much as we say we want to do things differently this time, it's easy to forget these vows when a new relationship begins. The excitement of discovering that there is life—and even love—after a breakup can eclipse our sense of who we are and what we want.

S-l-o-w down. Of course there's life and love after a breakup! And, if you've found both, that's great! *But you do not need to sacrifice yourself for it.* Remember when love got you to stop listening to your own music, or to miss chick-flick night with your girl-friends, and how you said you'd never do that again? We drop things we love because we feel "so lucky" to have a great relationship. It's as if we've met the quota on happiness and can't expect more. As one breakup survivor put it, "I get so taken in by a little bit of happiness, I take the whole package [of the relationship]." And when we take the whole package, we often leave ourselves behind. You need you, and for a real relationship, he needs you, too!

Sure, love instills a little temporary insanity. You want to gaze into each other's eyes, talk on the phone during the brief moments you're not together, and enjoy all that wonderfully nauseating stuff. Indulge—you deserve it! The danger comes when you think that you can't expect more.

We can develop a kind of superstition that, if it's good, we'd better not mess with it. For example, let's say that your new boyfriend wants to be with you as much as possible. That's great! But on chick-flick night, you want to be with your friends. But you decide you'd better not mess with his desire to be with you, and you cancel out on your friends. This choice is based on *scarcity thinking*, which tells you that you can only have one thing at the sacrifice of another.

Abundance thinking says you can have his desire to be with you AND your time with friends. And if his interest in being with you fades because of one evening apart, then he's not what you want anyway. More likely, absence will make his desire stronger, and then you'll have it all!

This may be the number-one challenge of dating again: to bring all of who you are, and all of your desires, to your relationships. When it comes to you, more is better! A person with more interests and more friends and more to give is generally more attractive than someone who just needs love. Which brings us back to loving ourselves. Perhaps it's appropriate to end this story with some insights from the fictional love (and sex) writer of *Sex and the City* fame, Carrie Bradshaw:

> *Later that day I got to thinking about relationships. There are those that open you up to something new and exotic, those that are old and familiar, those that bring up lots of questions, those that bring you somewhere unexpected, those that bring you far from where you started, and those that bring you back. But the most exciting, challenging, and significant relationship of all is the one you have with yourself. And if you find someone to love the you you love, well, that's just fabulous.*— (http://www.sexandthecityquotes.com)

The Least You Need to Know

- Create a ritual to help you let go.
- Practice seeing the humor in your life.
- Learn to watch and enjoy your own drama.
- Go alone to places where people you like gather.
- Don't let fluctuating feelings throw you off course.
- Do change course as your desires evolve.

Soothe-the-Blues Remedies

When we're feeling really down, sometimes we just want someone to tell us what to do. Here are a variety of prescriptions for the conditions we pick up after a breakup.

Be a friend. Shift your attention from your own problems and see how you can help. Lend a hand to a neighbor doing work in the yard. Bring your best friend lunch at work. Baby-sit for a new mom. Walk a dog. Tend to a sick relative. Giving of yourself helps you feel fuller and less needy.

Binge on trash-lit. Go to a grocery or drug store and pick up the trashiest celebrity literature you can find. Get a good selection, and then invite some friends over for a study group. Read to each other stories of celebrity breakups and scandals and see who can find the best one. Marvel at the fact that people with that much success are even more miserable than you!

Blog your mind. Join the universal conversation. Sign up with one of the many blog sites on the web and start sharing your personal insights and reflections.

Buy underwear. Whatever it is that you need but have neglected to buy for yourself, go out and get it. Sometimes it's the little things like underwear, dental floss, or vitamins that you neglect to restock. If your towels have gotten ratty, treat yourself to some thick new ones. Attending to the little things can be a wonderful expression of self-love.

Cinematherapy. Rent or go to a movie that helps you indulge your feelings. Check out Appendix C for some movie therapy prescriptions.

Clean. Some reward, huh? Yes! Cleaning your space to the level of shine you love is an expression of self-care and gives you a great sense of satisfaction and control. Scrubbing, sweeping, and dusting also provide great exercise!

(Or, hire a maid). If you're not up for a cleaning workout, employ a professional to do it for you. Pretend you do this all the time.

Create something. Artists, writers, and musicians know how to transform difficult feelings into beauty. Write a poem or a song; draw, paint, or sculpt; sing or play an instrument.

Cry. If you feel like crying, go ahead. A good cry releases built-up tension and clears the system. Pamper your crying self as a good mother would.

Declare your independence. Write a list of all the things you can do now that you weren't able to do when you were in a relationship. Maybe there are movies you've missed, invites you've declined, friends you've neglected. Think small about the little things that annoyed him that you can do without apology; think big about things like singles cruises and chance love encounters.

Embrace the space. Whether you have new digs, less of his stuff around, or fewer interruptions, indulge in the personal space. Drink in the quiet, meditate, putter.

Expand your mind. Sign up for that jazz history class you always wanted to take, research that awesome book idea you've been harboring, learn a new language, read a classic.

Get physical. Exercise is a very powerful anti-depressant as well as a great release for anger. (Punching bag, anyone?) Treat yourself to some cute workout attire and hit the road, courts, or the gym. Stretch, run, swim; hit the machines or a ball. Pour the intensity of your feelings into your workout.

Get a massage. Mmmm. Need I say more?

Get nurtured by nature. Take a hike in the woods. Meditate under the moonlight. Bask in the sun. Allow Mother Nature to soothe you with her gifts.

Get a pedicure. This rivals a massage for the self-indulgence factor. Foot massage, lotions, soaking— If you haven't had one, you'll never be the same.

Get out of town. Get in the car and get away. Road time can be great for thinking things through and getting perspective. As you gain physical distance, problems seem smaller and you notice a bigger world out there. You can return with new ideas and fresh energy.

Join. Meet people who share your interests. Whatever you enjoy, there's probably a club to match. If you crave exercise, try a running or biking group. If you love books, join a book club; cooking: gourmet club; writing: writers' group or poetry club; politics: pick a campaign; nature: Sierra Club; acting: community theatre. If the club you want isn't there, create it!

Laugh. Take a friend to a comedy club, read anything by David Sedaris or Sophie Kinsella, learn a new joke, hang out with funny people.

Pajama party. Get your mind off of boys and relish some girl-fun. Have your friends bring their dorkiest pajamas, sleeping bags, nail polish, makeup, hair-fixing supplies, music, movies, and munchies. Camp out in the living room—and, this time, Mom won't be telling you when to go to bed (we hope).

Pity party. Indulge yourself with a party where you can really cry if you want to. Invite your closest friends and ask them each to bring a box of tissue and a box of chocolate. Watch sad movies, set up a dart board with the ex's photo on it, share "worst breakup" stories, and give a prize to the best one.

Play with dirt. Get out in your garden and dig! Working the earth can feel very grounding. Feel the satisfaction of pulling weeds and planting good stuff—a useful metaphor for your dating life!

Relish the time. Read that book your best friend recommended, take up tai chi or pottery, do the thing you didn't have time for when you were in the relationship.

Renew your spirit. Go to your church, synagogue, or temple. Talk to a spiritual director or take a yoga retreat. Connect with other seekers and open yourself to greater sources of renewal.

Repair things. Maybe you can't fix the relationship that broke, but you can take care of some other things. Sew that button back on your shirt; call the plumber about the drip under the sink; glue the handle back on your favorite mug. Enjoy the satisfaction of making things whole and complete.

Put your breakup to music. Soothe yourself with the voices of those who have suffered this, too. Indulge in your favorite music at home or expose yourself to new sounds in a live setting. Have friends share their favorite breakup songs.

Spa at home. Prep your bathroom with soothing music, candles, yummy-smelling bubble bath, lotion, washcloths, fluffy towels, and a bath robe. If you want to go exotic, prepare yourself a cocktail. Immerse yourself in the warmth of the water and, if tears flow, there's plenty of water to wash them away.

Tell your story. Hook up with a therapist or breakup support group and feel the healing power of having a witness (or witnesses) to your journey.

Volunteer. A great way to get out of yourself is to help others who are suffering. Volunteer at an animal shelter or a soup kitchen. Pick up groceries for the old lady down the street. Besides giving you good feelings, volunteering helps you feel connected and put your own problems into perspective.

Write the unsendable. Write a letter to your ex telling him exactly what you feel. Spare nothing: this is your time to purge. Tell him about everything you're going through, attack his personality and his fashion sense, confess all the love you still feel—whatever is there, put it down. Get it all out of you and on the paper. Then shred it all or burn it.

Write your story. Whether you record your feelings in a journal or formally write your breakup memoirs, the act of writing is a powerful release and great therapy. Transform your problem into good literature.

Better Words for Bad Situations

The way we talk to ourselves can either make things better or much, much worse. Use the examples below to substitute mean and discouraging lies with helpful, calming, and more accurate statements. If the "better" statements don't satisfy you, take the "leap of faith."

***

Lie: *I'll never find what I'm looking for.*

Better: *The world can change in a day. I don't know what's going to happen.*

Leap of Faith: *There are possibilities beyond my imagination. Life has just opened the way to serendipity.*

***

Lie: *I can't stand this!*

Better: *This is hard, but I can stand it. I have strengths that will help me through.*

Leap of Faith: *It's darkest before the dawn.*

***

Lie: *This shouldn't be happening to me.*

Better: *I wish this wasn't happening, but I can face it.*

Leap of Faith: *What's happening now is an essential part of my story.*

***

Lie: *I'm a loser.*

Better: *I'm hurting, but I'm not a loser. Maybe I didn't see the signs, but I can learn from this.*

Leap of Faith: *I'm a winner going through trials that will make me even better.*

***

Lie: *All men are jerks.*

Better: *Some men—like my ex—are jerks, but there are great guys, too.*

Leap of Faith: *The best is yet to come!*

***

Lie: *I should have seen this coming.*

Better: *I am now better at seeing signs. I wish I had seen them then, but I forgive myself.*

Leap of Faith: *I had valid reasons for trusting him. I needed to go through the process, and even though it hurt, it has helped me sort everything out.*

***

Lie: *I'm not attractive*

Better: *I'm not attractive to everybody—no one is. I attracted my ex, and I'll attract others.*

Leap of Faith: *I am just what some guys are looking for. I'll not only attract somebody, I'll wow him!*

***

Lie: *I'm not loveable.*

Better: *My ex does not determine my lovability.*

Leap of Faith: *I was lovable as a tiny baby and I couldn't do anything then. Look at all I've added to that already-amazing creature!*

***

Lie: *I'm going crazy!*

Better: *I'm feeling confused and anxious right now, but this is temporary.*

Leap of Faith: *This is beyond my understanding right now, but the world is conspiring in my favor.*

***

Lie: *I'm pathetic!*

Better: *I'm hurting, but that doesn't make me pathetic.*

Leap of Faith: *I'm feeling so much because of my depth and capacity for love. When I meet my match, it's going to be epic!*

***

Lie: *I'm a ball-breaking bitch.*

Better: *I'm powerful.* [Or] *Just because he has no balls doesn't make me a bitch!*

Leap of Faith: *I won't reduce myself or my standards. Next time, I'll find someone who can rise to the challenge.*

***

Lie: *I'm selfish.*

Better: *I care about myself, and anyone who loves me will applaud that!*

Leap of Faith: *I am good to myself and I'm excited to find someone who loves that about me and is good to me, too!*

***

Lie: *I'm a failure.*

Better: *Maybe this relationship didn't work out, but what is success anyway?*

Leap of Faith: *Look at all the famous people who suffered repeated failures along the way. I'm not giving up either!*

***

Lie: *I'm too emotional.*

Better: *I'm emotional because I have a heart.*

Leap of Faith: *I'd rather feel everything than to close my heart. And when I feel joy, it will be as intense as this!*

***

Lie: *They always leave in the end.*

Better: *I don't know what will happen in the future. Anything is possible!*

Leap of Faith: *It only takes one to make the world turn upside down. I believe in upside down!*

***

Lie: *I'm too clingy/dependent/needy.*

Better: *We all need people. I value closeness and intimacy. It's love that makes life rich.*

Leap of Faith: *There is a wealth of love in this world, and those who ask for it are much more likely to get it!*

***

Lie: *When they get to know me they leave.*

Better: *I don't know how this story will turn out. Even if every guy so far has left, that does not tell me what will happen tomorrow.*

Leap of Faith: *The world can change in a day, and so can this script.*

***

Lie: *I'm dull/boring/forgettable.*

Better: *So I'm not on drugs or into S&M.*

Leap of Faith: *If someone sees me as dull, they don't know me. When the eyes of love fall on me, the qualities that make me unique and exciting will glow like sequins under a spotlight.*

***

Lie: *Men only want me for the sex.*

Better: *Jerks only want me for the sex, and I don't want them!*

Leap of Faith: *I'm not apologizing for being sexy or for enjoying my sexuality. I have a right to my attractiveness as well as my depth, and the lucky guys will see both.*

***

Lie: *I'm not feminine/nurturing enough.*

Better: *I'm not his mother, but that's okay 'cause I'm not into boys.*

Leap of Faith: *I am enough just the way I am. I'm not for everybody—I'm an individual. And this individual is somebody special!*

***

Lie: *I'm too fat/ugly.*

Better: *Beauty is in the eye of the beholder, and I just need a new beholder!*

Leap of Faith: *I'm worthy of being seen, held, and adored like everyone else. Nothing and nobody can diminish that.*

***

Lie: *I'm too competitive.*

Better: *I like a challenge!*

Leap of Faith: *I'm good, and I just need someone who can rise to the challenge. Good times two will be great!*

***

Lie: *I'm too*   [fill in the blank]   .

Better: *I may have too much* _____ *for my ex, but the next guy might love that about me!*

Leap of Faith: *My "too much" is my specialty—it's what I do best. It's my gift to the world, and I'm not going to hide it!*

Lie: *I'm too*   [fill in the blank]   .

Better: *I may have too much* _____ *for my ex, but the next guy might love that about me!*

Leap of Faith: *My "too much" is my specialty—it's what I do best. It's my gift to the world, and I'm not going to hide it!*

Movie Therapy Prescriptions

About a Boy (2002)
Hugh Grant
Nicholas Hoult
Toni Collette

Provides humorous insight into men and boys, how they relate and mature. A good alternative to the standard chick flick, still revealing the transforming power of love.

Will (Grant): In my opinion, all men are islands. And what's more, now's the time to be one. This is an island age.

An Affair to Remember (1957)
Cary Grant
Deborah Kerr

Classic romance that had Meg Ryan's character captivated in "Sleepless in Seattle" and was listed #5 on the American Film Institute's list of 100 Greatest Love Stories. Get caught up in a shipboard romance that seems both magical and impossible.

Nickie Ferrante (Grant): There must be something between us, even if it's only an ocean.

Casablanca (1942)
Humphrey Bogart
Ingrid Bergman

The number-one greatest love story, according to
the American Film Institute. Feel the tension of
Isla's (Bergman) escape attempt from German held
Morocco, as Rick (Bogart) decides whether and
how to challenge the police, the Nazis and his own
bitter feelings to assist Ilsa and the resistance leader
Lazlo. The movie's emotional range is broad and
heart wrenching.

Ilsa: Play it once, Sam. For old times' sake.

Sam: [lying] I don't know what you mean, Miss Ilsa.

Ilsa: Play it, Sam. Play "As Time Goes By."

Charade (1963)
Cary Grant
Audrey Hepburn

Romantic Parisian mystery full of twists and snappy
dialogue. Lots of fun in a movie that helps answer
the question of why Audrey Hepburn's style and
personality are so beguiling. A real escape that will
get you smiling.

Peter Joshua (Grant): Reggie, cut it out.

Reggie Lampert (Hepburn): Okay.

Peter: Well, now what are you doing?

Reggie: Cutting it out.

Peter: Who told you to do that?

Down with Love (2003)
Renee Zellweger
Ewan McGregor
David Hyde Pierce

A takeoff on the Doris Day-Rock Hudson dynamic, with David Hyde Pierce handling Tony Randall's role masterfully. Lots of sexual innuendo and '60s posh eye candy. Fun and entertaining.

Narrator: The place: New York City. The time: Now, 1962. And there's no time or place like it. If you've got a dream, this is the place to make that dream come true. That's why the soaring population of hopeful dreamers has just reached eight million people. Oh! Make that eight million and one.

Eternal Sunshine of the Spotless Mind (2004)
Jim Carrey
Kate Winslet

Imaginative and bizarre, this movie throws out puzzle pieces and craftily brings them together. Reveals how love is built on memories, and wrestles with the dilemma of whether to stay in the fire of a relationship. Nice soundtrack. Great movie for inspiring reflection.

Clementine (Winslet): This is it, Joel. It's going to be gone soon.

Joel (Carrey): I know.

Clementine: What do we do?

Joel: Enjoy it.

Garden State (2004)
Zach Braff
Natalie Portman

Funny and familiar sense of revisiting high school party culture, alienation, sadness, emotional intimacy, and real connection. Awesome soundtrack. Theme of choosing life with all its feeling. Great food for reflection.

Sam (Portman): Are you really retarded?

Andrew Largeman (Braff): No.

Sam: Ooh, great job, man! I really thought you were retarded. I mean, you're better than that Corky kid, and he's actually retarded. If there was a retarded Oscar, you would win, hands down, kick his ass!

Groundhog Day (1993)
Andie MacDowell
Bill Murray

Hopeful, funny, and surprisingly philosophical. Looks at the challenge of changing our steps in the relationship dance. A movie that celebrates that change can happen in a day—as long as that day repeats itself endlessly.

Phil (Murray): Something is … different.

Rita (MacDowell): Good or bad?

Phil: Anything different is good.

Hitch (2005)
Will Smith
Eva Mendes
Jeffrey Donovan

Guy flick for chicks (and guys). It's fun to see the extremely cool male character go neurotic when love hits. There are some great role-reversals here, and the movie combines the heart of romantic comedy with the edgy humor more characteristic of guy movies. The mood is generally light and fun, yet will leave you with that after-movie glow us chicks love.

Vance (Donovan): [after telling Hitch that he only wants a girl so he can sleep with her] No, I was told that you help guys get in there.

Alex 'Hitch' Hitchens (Smith): Right, but see, here's the thing - my clients actually like *women. "Hit it and quit it" is not my thing.*

Junebug (2005)
Embeth Davidtz
Alessandro Nivola
Amy Adams

Delightful. The chemistry between Madeleine, with her British accent and worldly charm, and guy-next-door George, bring them on a spontaneous visit to his family in North Carolina. Amy Adams, adorable as George's pregnant and ceaselessly cheerful sister-in-law, was nominated for an Oscar for her supporting role. She's an inspiration to anyone who's had it rough. You will want to take her home.

Madeleine (Davidtz): I was born in Japan.
Ashley (Adams): You were not!

Moonstruck (1987)
Cher
Nicholas Cage
Olympia Dukakas
Vincent Gardenia

Quirky, funny, dramatic, and warm. Sensual qualities abound, from Cher's gorgeous curly locks, to the blissful music of *La Bohème*, to the oversized moon in the Manhattan sky. Nicholas Cage and Olympia Dukakas are hilarious.

Rose (Dukakas): Do you love him, Loretta?

Loretta (Cher): No.

Rose: Good. [She looks at Cosmo (Gardenia).] When you love them, they drive you crazy because they know they can.

My Best Friend's Wedding (1997)
Julia Roberts
Dermot Mulroney
Cameron Diaz
Rupert Everett

Funny, suspenseful, at times maddening, and ultimately thought-provoking. Sometimes what counts is the love that picks you up when love is lost. Julia Roberts and Cameron Diaz make great comic counterparts, and Rupert Everett is charming, witty, and frustratingly gorgeous as her gay friend and editor.

Julianne Potter (Roberts): I'm pond scum. Well, lower actually. I'm like the fungus that feeds on pond scum.

Michael O'Neal (Mulroney): Lower. The pus that infects the mucus that cruds up the fungus that feeds on the pond scum. On the other hand, thank you for loving me that much, that way. It's pretty flattering.

Julianne Potter (Roberts): Except it makes me fungus.

My Big Fat Greek Wedding (2002)
Nia Vardalos
John Corbett

Nia Vardalos is loveable as the shy and awkward 30-year-old who is becoming the source of her parents' anxiety because she is unmarried. John Corbett is the hot non-Greek who messes with the family agenda. The maddening and loveable aspects of family are tossed together with lots of Greek food in a flick that might just cast your own family in a more endearing light. The mood ranges from intimate and tender to hilarious to just plain joyful.

Toula Portokalo (Vardalos): I had to go to Greek school, where I learned valuable lessons such as, "If Nick has one goat and Maria has nine, how soon will they marry?"

Phat Girlz (2006)
Mo'Nique
Kendra C. Johnson
Jimmy Jean-Louis

Though not a critic's favorite, this portrait of a woman in a losing battle with weight brings a refreshing perspective to our cultural biases about attractiveness. Although she leads with her sense of humor, Mo'Nique's performance is notable for her portrayal of the pain and self-hatred that can accompany life in a larger size. See your own perception of beauty change as the movie progresses.

Jazmin Biltmore (Mo'Nique): I hate skinny bitches

Pillow Talk (1959)
Doris Day
Rock Hudson
Tony Randall

A classic Doris Day and Rock Hudson formula film, with neurotic sidekick Tony Randall. A visual playground of '60s style and color, an almost-farcical portrayal of sexual banter and dating games.

Jan (Day): Officer, arrest this man—he's taking me up to his apartment!

Police Officer: Well, I can't say that I blame him, miss.

Pretty Woman (1990)
Julia Roberts
Richard Gere

Cinderella story with humor, tenderness, a great revenge scene, and the vulnerability that made Julia Roberts so loveable. Appeals to the girl in all of us.

Shop assistant: Hello, can I help you?

Vivian (Roberts): I was in here yesterday. You wouldn't wait on me.

Shop assistant: Oh.

Vivian: You people work on commission, right?

Shop assistant: Yeah.

Vivian: Big mistake. Big. Huge. I have to go shopping now.

Roxanne (1987)
Steve Martin
Daryl Hannah

Based on the play *Cyrano de Bergerac*, large-nosed C.D. Bales falls for the stunning Roxanne, and she loves his personality but another man's looks. Sweet and intelligent, the characters make you reconsider what is attractive.

C.D. Bales (Martin): I said, "Ten more seconds and I'm leaving!" Wait a second! What did you think I said?

Roxanne (Hannah): I thought you said, "Earn more sessions by sleeving."

C.D. Bales: Well, what the hell does that mean?

Roxanne: I don't know. That's why I came out.

Sabrina (1954 version)
Audrey Hepburn
Humphrey Bogart
William Holden

Who cannot love Audrey Hepburn in this charming role? Top it off with Humphrey Bogart and William Holden, and you've got magic. The 1995 remake with Julia Ormond, Harrison Ford, and Greg Kinnear is also good. The story is uplifting; makes you believe anything can happen.

Sabrina Fairchild (Hepburn): Oh, but Paris isn't for changing planes. It's for changing your outlook. For throwing open the windows and letting in … letting in la vie en rose.*

**[a French saying meaning "life is rosy"]*

Shopgirl (2005)
Claire Danes
Steve Martin
Jason Schwartzman

Quirky, great characters, leaves you in a good yet bittersweet, reflective place.

Mirabelle (Danes): Are you the kind of person that takes time to get to know, and then once you get to know them…they're fabulous?

Jeremy (Schwartzman): Yes, absolutely. … What?

Sleepless in Seattle (1993)
Meg Ryan
Tom Hanks
Ross Malinger

A classic romantic comedy that inspires you to believe in love after the loss of love, in the ability of a child to heal an adult, and in the possibility of serendipity. Mood moves ranges from somber to funny to romantic.

Sam Baldwin (Hanks): I am NOT going to New York to meet some woman who could be a crazy, sick lunatic! Didn't you see Fatal Attraction?

The Upside of Anger (2005)
Joan Allen
Kevin Costner

Angry and funny. If you want someone to mirror your rage over being left or cheated on (or both), Joan Allen's character will do the job. Mostly reveals the downside of anger, but there's a lesson to be learned.

Lavender "Popeye" Wolfmeyer [daughter]: Anger and resentment can stop you in your tracks. That's what I know now. It needs nothing to burn but the air and the life that it swallows and smothers. It's real, though—the fury, even when it isn't. It can change you ... turn you ... mold you and shape you into something you're not. The only upside to anger, then ... is the person you become.

Tips for Good Fighting

Good fighting refers to what happens when two people bring their desires into their interactions. Relationships get stale when partners begin to withhold their deepest desires and ultimate dreams from each other. Here are some ways to promote good fighting:

Keep it safe. Of course, this means there is no threat of physical aggression. But this also means that behaviors that *feel* threatening can be discussed and limited. For example, you may need to say, "When you raise your voice like that I feel intimidated," and wait for your partner to tone it down.

Good fighting requires a balance of power that enables both partners to influence the direction of the conversation. If you can't find that balance, then you're not only in a bad fight—you're in a bad relationship.

Make it a good match. Negotiate how you fight. Notice and confront behaviors that close you or your partner down. Yelling, threats, insults, even silence, diminish good fighting.

Fight for I and we. Fighting for both means saying: "This is really important to me, *and* our relationship is really important to me. How can we make this work for both of us?"

Bring desire, not deprivation. Tell your partner what you want, not how you've been deprived. Stay committed to having more for you and for the relationship. When these two desires conflict, get creative!

Don't wait for him to figure it out. He won't. Use words. Tell him. It's not his job to read your mind. It's your job to express your feelings and needs.

Fight for small things. Don't dismiss your desires as trivial or silly. Ask him to brush your hair as you watch the game; tell him you like when he brings you coffee in the morning.

Help your partner fight you. When he attacks your desire or disengages, find out what he wants. Open up the conflict that your partner is closing off. Remember: You are fighting for both-and, not either-or.

Don't agree too quickly. Halfhearted agreements do not hold. Before agreeing, share your resistance: "I'm wanting to do this for you, but if I don't get this addressed, I'm afraid I won't follow through."

Make room for fighting. Take the time to share what you're wanting out of life. Negotiate your sexual desires. Anticipate and talk about what kind of weekend you are each wanting.

Allow multiple rounds. The best part of a good fight is what happens between conversations, when you each reflect on what the other person said. Real differences don't resolve in a single round, ending with a neat "I'm sorry" and a loving embrace. The good fight is an ongoing commitment to being alive and present in the relationship. Every resolved round brings you to a new level of intimacy and personal growth. Why would you want this kind of fight to end?

Let go of the outcome. Let good fighting be a discovery process. Fight with vigor, expect good things, and practice not knowing what the outcome will be. You will be pleasantly surprised.

Stay in fighting shape. Fighting requires energy. Gear up by gaining support from friends, clarifying what you want, and taking yourself seriously.

Celebrate success. When he meets your desire, say thanks! Reveal your excitement. Give each other the gift of your pleasure and gratitude.

Index